FROM HANDS

WI

Best wishes to Pam,

Ariel Price

December 2018

DEBBIE YOUNG – Author of the 'Sophie Sayers Village Mysteries' and Director of the Hawkesbury Upton Literature Festival.
'. . . intriguing, compelling and moving. It was interesting at many levels – as a social history of both civilian life and services life, and as a microcosm of the love, hope and heartbreak caused by the war . . . could potentially make a great radio play or spoken word performance.'

SUZIE GROGAN – Author of 'Shell Shocked Britain' and 'Death, Disease and Dissection'.
'Just a quick look has piqued my interest . . . the ingredients of a wonderful book . . . put all together in a way that does all those fabulous sources, and the love story, justice.'

CATHERINE SAMPSON – Social and Family Historian based in Berkshire.
'The synopsis alone had me 'hooked' by the lure of both surviving letters and diaries, the latter being relatively rare from the front line as they were banned, and also the additional activities of 'Gran' and her singing troupe. Congratulations on an excellent account of a relationship during the so called Great War.'

FROM HANDSWORTH TO HEBRON WITH THE HEREFORDS

1917 *Diary and Letters*

Amiel Price

Fronheulog Books
2018

First published by Fronheulog Books in 2018

Available from Amiel Price
Telephone: 01792 369121

ISBN 978-1-9164280-0-3

Back Cover Illustrations:

The watercolour title - V.A.D. *Moor Green Hall*, 1917.
Taken from Amiel's autograph album which accompanied autographs of Brett, Warren and Povey.

Flags of the Allied countries hand painted on silk.

Amiel in her flag costume.

The author with her mother in 2012 watching the Olympic Torch relay, Mumbles.

Printed and bound in Wales by
Dinefwr Print & Design
Rawlings Road, Llandybie
Carmarthenshire, SA18 3YD

This book is dedicated to the memory
of Norman Wells, Amiel Robins
and my late parents Maureen and John Price

CONTENTS

ACKNOWLEDGEMENTS

I have first to thank my Grandmother and Mother for keeping safe this rich archive of letters, diaries and photographs for a hundred years. What started out as a little book to share with close family members has become a full scale published book to share with the wider world. For this I can only thank my friends for their independent interest and encouragement – Cheryl, Liz, Debbie, Suzie, and Catherine. I must thank Fiona Tait, former archivist at City of Birmingham Library, who was fascinated when I showed her the diaries and photos for digitising and gave me the added incentive from a professional historian. Particular thanks go to Bridget O'Callaghan for her helpful and detailed feedback and to Paulette Burkill, Secretary of the Handsworth Historical Society for her local knowledge and editorial contribution. And thanks to my brother and our late father for listening to me going on about it all for so long.

FOREWORD

The importance of personal experience to the lasting record and commemoration of war cannot be underestimated. The impact of conflict on the lives of individuals resonates with us in a way that an overview of the period, however fascinating, never can. Social history, dealing with the minutiae of daily life, even at its seemingly most mundane, takes the reader back in time and offers them the opportunity to be part of the story. We can sit with the protagonists and almost be part of their world, living through quiet triumphs and heart-breaking tragedy alike.

The Great War is a period in the history of Great Britain that has left a lasting legacy on us all. It altered British society forever and led to changes that, just a few years before its ending in 1918, would have been unimaginable. It is important that we record and recognise the impact, especially as we approach the commemoration of the end of the war in 2018, and the beginning of the 'legacy' – the coping, the grieving, the adjusting and the moving on from the devastating events of 1914-1918.

Diaries, letters and photographs are an invaluable historical resource. They offer us the opportunity to all but hear the voices of those, often long dead, who penned them hardly imagining that they would be of interest to anyone but themselves. Making the decision to publish and make public this highly personal material is not easy, but in the case of the letters and diary entries in this book it is clear that sharing their story is nothing but a tribute to the love between two young people and the impact the Great War had on their lives. Amiel Price, in her introduction, also highlights how often the challenges faced by British troops in Egypt and Palestine are overlooked as history focuses on the horrors of the Western Front. This book plays a significant part in readdressing the balance.

Norman Wells expresses the hopes and fears of many of the young men of the time, thousands of miles away from loved ones in a different world. His letters are expressive not only of a love for his Amiel, the author's maternal grandmother whose diary entries suggest she was a middle-class girl of considerable charm, but also of life, landscape and the belief in a future free of war.

SUZIE GROGAN
Author of *Shell Shocked Britain* and *Death, Disease and Dissection.*

PREFACE

In 2014 I returned to my home town of Swansea to clear out the parental home in Langland Bay following the death of my mother. Whilst sorting through the cupboards and drawers, all full of assorted treasures from several generations, I discovered a box of love letters dating from 1917.

These were letters written to my maternal grandmother Amiel Robins from her fiancé Norman Wells. They both lived in Birmingham – in Handsworth and neighbouring Birchfield. Gradually as I read the letters I was drawn into their story, particularly as they were accompanied by some lovely black and white photographs and some rather humorous cartoons drawn by Norman. There were no letters found from Amiel to Norman, but I did discover a tiny diary of hers for 1917 and a notebook in which she had copied out the last three months of that year from Norman's diary. His letters cover the period from when he was training to become an officer to the period when he was part of the Egypt Expeditionary Force.

I didn't expect to find any connection with Wales at all so I was surprised to discover that in July 1917 Norman's battalion came to a camp in Singleton Park, Swansea. His letters describe walks to Mumbles and Langland Bay and going to a Gala in Victoria Park where medals were being awarded to Welsh soldiers.

With the commemoration of the First World War drawing to a close, I felt it was important to make my own contribution by publishing this story, not only because it portrays a poignant love story and gives a flavour of a way of life now long gone, but because it gives an insight into an overlooked campaign away from the Western Front.

INTRODUCTION

Amiel Robins lived with her parents Lewis and 'Tiny' Robins at 191 Holly Road, Handsworth, Birmingham. She was born on 7th February in 1897, so had her twentieth birthday in 1917. As part of her war effort she joined the National and Provincial Bank in Bennett's Hill, Birmingham, where she wrote up all the ledgers. She was always busiest during 'The Balance' at the end of each month, often working late into the evening. I remember my mother always telling me that she had beautiful copperplate handwriting. It may have been through the Bank that she met Norman because he had also worked there in the past, and he often refers to the Bank and the people there and of her keeping his job for him. But however it was, they met in December 1916 just before Christmas. He says in the first letter that has survived, dated 29th December 1916, that she must not let on that they only met a week ago.

From her diaries you get a feel of the kind of life she led – she made the occasional hat or sewed a camisole, went ice skating or played tennis with friends, and with her mother (referred to as M in the diary) went to Gilbert and Sullivan shows and even the Turkish Baths! Her father (referred to as F) played cards and billiards with his friends at home – we still had the very billiard balls until just recently. And of course she describes the lovely times with Norman when they went walking, having tea or visiting the picture houses (cinemas). But the stories I'd heard from my mother were that Amiel sang with a troupe of girls who called themselves 'The Allies'.

This was a bit different! From her diary you can see references to the rehearsals and to a Mr Griffin, who I think was their Musical Director. The real Allies during WW1 were of course the countries who joined forces against Germany. There's a group photograph of the girls in costumes representing each one of these countries. They put on concerts and entertainments mainly in military hospitals and convalescent homes around Birmingham but also in other halls and in the Birmingham Botanical Gardens. Her diary mentions several places, such as Churchfields in West Bromwich, Monyhull in Kings Norton, Selly Oak, and Camp Sutton amongst others. A Birmingham newspaper, with a photo of the girls dressed as a football team called

'The Hotspurs', said that 'these Birmingham girls have given a hundred performances at entertainments to wounded soldiers'.

Incidentally, organised male football was suspended during the war and the FA Cup Final of 1915 was the last one for five years. However, as more and more women took over men's roles in munitions factories and other industrial works, they also took the opportunity to form their own football teams within their factories. By 1917 women's football had become very popular and the Munitionettes Cup had been established.

Norman Albert Wells was 26 years old when he met Amiel. He was the only child of Albert and Beatrice Wells and they lived in 12 Trinity Road (and previously 53 Hampton Road) Birchfield, Birmingham, not far from Handsworth. He was an accomplished singer and also played the piano. He was 'well known in local musical circles having been a member of the Birchfield Amateur Operatic Society for several years and taking the leading roles in many operas that they had staged'. As seen in his letters, he refers to taking part in concerts during his time in the army, and he often sent Amiel song sheets, some of which have survived to this day.

When war broke out he was in the service of the National and Provincial Bank (originally in Birmingham but at some point he was in the Hereford branch), and as soon as it was possible to release him he joined and attained the rank of sergeant-major after twelve months service.

His earliest letters to Amiel cover the period when he is an officer cadet in Newmarket, Suffolk. They had only recently met and it must have been very difficult to woo a girl from a distance. It's interesting to follow how the tone changes in the way he addresses her in his letters and how he describes his feelings for her and persuades her to write frequently and tell him how she feels.

Once gazetted, he is in Oswestry as a Second Lieutenant with the Herefordshire Regiment – in which all units were of the Territorial Force (now known as the Territorial Army). He longs for leave when he can spend time with Amiel back in Handsworth, but it's her diary that fills the gap and tells us how they spent their time together – walking in Sutton Park, visiting the Botanical Gardens, going to picture houses and cafés.

Amiel and Norman became engaged on 26th May when she and her mother visited him at Oswestry Park Hall Camp, staying at Whittington nearby. During this time Norman actually writes in Amiel's diary – writing as if he were she. Later on he writes very amusingly of the horse riding lessons he undergoes. He illustrates this with cartoons to show the kind of tricks they have to perform to get used to the feel of the horse. Each time is with a different horse and you realise that a city lad has to be able to handle any horse he is given to ride when an officer in the army.

Once in Egypt and Palestine his letters describe how desperate he is to hear from Amiel and you realise that three or four weeks go by before the first letters reach him, and presumably vice versa. His letters become very descriptive of the foreign land and the unusual sights and peoples he sees, but also are solicitous and full of hope, looking forward to when they can be together forever at last.

There are some gaps in the letters and a few explanatory paragraphs have been added in places, but the letters are beautifully written so they have been left to tell their own story.

PART I:

EARLY DAYS

Norman Wells.

Try to let me have that photo please!

HUT No. 13 B COY.,
No. 13 OFFICER CADET BATTn.,
NEWMARKET.

29th Decr 1916.

My dear Amiel,

I hope you won't mind having another letter from me so soon but I have done all the work I intend to do tonight & it is too wet & too late to go out so I thought I would send a few lines as there is hardly anyone I write to except to home.

We arrived here quite safely at 5.30, the train was 4½ hours late, but we didn't mind as we managed to get a good feed at Bletchley & tea at Cambridge. When we got to Newmarket we had another meal & then

First Letter.

Friday 29th Dec 1916
Hut No. 13, B Company
No.13 Officer Cadet Battalion
Newmarket [Suffolk]

My dear Amiel,

I hope you won't mind having another letter from me so soon but I have done all the work I intend to do tonight and it is too wet and too late to go out so I thought I would send a few lines as there is hardly anyone I write to except to home.

We arrived here quite safely at 5.30, the train was 4 1/2 hours late, but we didn't mind as we managed to get a good feed at Bletchley and tea at Cambridge. When we got to Newmarket we had another meal and then went to the pictures where I saw my old pal Charlie Chaplin. I did wish you could have been with me as it was awfully good, and I couldn't help thinking of the last time we were at the pictures.

Today has been fearfully cold but now it is raining and it may get warmer, which we all hope for now, it is not pleasant having to stand about and freeze.

I suppose you are still in the office, it is just 9 o'clock, and I wish I could look in to give you a hand for half an hour; we might try to discover my name in the safe if you weren't too busy.

If by any chance you should meet my folks or anyone who knows them don't let on that we have only known each other for a week as I told Mother I had known you some time. I can't explain why I did so now but when I do you will quite understand, I said I had known you some months and I consider I have, seeing that you have been at the office so long. I know it is not a very clear or conclusive argument but you will see the reason when I next see you.

I wonder when I shall get home again, it does seem so rotten for us to be so far away when we could be so much happier together, at least I am sure I should be were I nearer you, and I hope you would be. Anyway, we seemed to get on very well and there didn't seem any immediate signs of a quarrel when I left, did there?

This epistle is about the longest I have written for years and I hope you are not very bored with reading it. Please write as soon and as often as you can, although I am not expecting a lot during balance week. I will write whenever I can, that is if you wish and I hope you do.

~~W~~ Yours very sincerely, Norman
I nearly put 'with love' but I suppose such short acquaintance hardly allows of such a thing.
Try to let me have that photo please!

2nd Jan 1917
Newmarket

My dear Amiel,

Very many thanks for your cheery letter. I seemed to have to wait a long time for it, but I suppose the Balance has kept you fairly well occupied during the last few days. At any rate perhaps you will write sooner the next time as I do look forward to hearing from you as you are the only girl I write to – honestly!

I am glad you would like me to be home again, but I am sorry I can't oblige just yet but my rib seems much easier now, in fact it is almost well. You may be sure I shall come to see you as soon as I possibly can, but don't forget there is a war on and we all have to give up something. Just write often and I will do the same and that is the best we can do at present. You seem very suspicious of me that I don't mean what I put in my letters; now please don't be like that. I don't make it a rule to take every girl I meet to the pictures and I am sure I should not have come to your house had I intended to forget you as soon as I came back here.

You don't mention about the photo, now do please try to get it for me, as a special favour. Mr Davidson sent me one of the group at the Bank and it is quite a nice one of you, but I should prefer the one you have at home.

We had a concert here last night at which I gave a few songs, one being *The Drum Major*. [published 1907].

Why did you not wish to come to the station? I suppose it is a difficulty to ask at the Bank for time off. I know it was in my time, but I am sure Father would have liked to have met you. I am very sorry you object to me sending 'love' at such short ac-

Photo of staff outside the Bank.
Amiel is 3rd row from the front, and 3rd lady from the right.

quaintance, but I really meant it, and nowadays we don't have the opportunities we used to have in peace times of being together a lot so letters have to be a substitute for walks and you will see I have sent it again. I did mean what I said so don't say rotten things about my not meaning it.

Give my best wishes to your Mother and Father and please write as soon as you can as I shall be looking out for it – don't wait until Saturday to write if you can possibly send it before.

I hope the Balance is nearly over and that you feel none the worse for it, I know it is a rotten job, I used to get very fed up with it. My cold is quite well now and I am much more fit than when at home, I only wish you were nearer here so that I could see you occasionally but wars can't be helped can they?

With love, Yours very sincerely, Norman.

PS I have a song I am sending you tomorrow, I can't send it tonight as I am not going to the Post Office and our letter box here is too small, so look out for it.

CALENDAR 1917.

JANUARY.						
S	...	7	14	21	28	...
M	1	8	15	22	29	...
Tu	2	9	16	23	30	...
W	3	10	17	24	31	...
Th	4	11	18	25	...	...
F	5	12	19	26	...	...
S	6	13	20	27	...	...

FEBRUARY.						
S	...	4	11	18	25	...
M	...	5	12	19	26	...
Tu	...	6	13	20	27	...
W	...	7	14	21	28	...
Th	1	8	15	22	...	...
F	2	9	16	23	...	...
S	3	10	17	24	...	...

MARCH.						
S	...	4	11	18	25	...
M	...	5	12	19	26	...
Tu	...	6	13	20	27	...
W	...	7	14	21	28	...
Th	1	8	15	22	29	...
F	2	9	16	23	30	...
S	3	10	17	24	31	...

APRIL.						
S	1	8	15	22	29	...
M	2	9	16	23	30	...
Tu	3	10	17	24	...	...
W	4	11	18	25	...	...
Th	5	12	19	26	...	...
F	6	13	20	27	...	...
S	7	14	21	28	...	...

MAY.						
S	...	6	13	20	27	...
M	...	7	14	21	28	...
Tu	1	8	15	22	29	...
W	2	9	16	23	30	...
Th	3	10	17	24	31	...
F	4	11	18	25	...	...
S	5	12	19	26	...	...

JUNE.						
S	...	3	10	17	24	...
M	...	4	11	18	25	...
Tu	...	5	12	19	26	...
W	...	6	13	20	27	...
Th	...	7	14	21	28	...
F	1	8	15	22	29	...
S	2	9	16	23	30	...

JULY.						
S	1	8	15	22	29	...
M	2	9	16	23	30	...
Tu	3	10	17	24	31	...
W	4	11	18	25	...	...
Th	5	12	19	26	...	...
F	6	13	20	27	...	...
S	7	14	21	28		...

AUGUST.						
S	...	5	12	19	26	...
M	...	6	13	20	27	...
Tu	...	7	14	21	28	...
W	1	8	15	22	29	...
Th	2	9	16	23	30	...
F	3	10	17	24	31	...
S	4	11	18	25	...	...

SEPTEMBER.						
S	...	2	9	16	23	30
M	...	3	10	17	24	...
Tu	...	4	11	18	25	...
W	...	5	12	19	26	...
Th	...	6	13	20	27	...
F	...	7	14	21	28	...
S	1	8	15	22	29	...

OCTOBER.						
S	...	7	14	21	28	...
M	1	8	15	22	29	...
Tu	2	9	16	23	30	...
W	3	10	17	24	31	...
Th	4	11	18	25	...	...
F	5	12	19	26	...	...
S	6	13	20	27	...	...

NOVEMBER.						
S	...	4	11	18	25	...
M	...	5	12	19	26	...
Tu	...	6	13	20	27	...
W	...	7	14	21	28	...
Th	1	8	15	22	29	...
F	2	9	16	23	30	...
S	3	10	17	24	...	...

DECEMBER.						
S	...	2	9	16	23	30
M	...	3	10	17	24	31
Tu	...	4	11	18	25	...
W	...	5	12	19	26	...
Th	...	6	13	20	27	...
F	...	7	14	21	28	...
S	1	8	15	22	29	...

Charles Letts's

SELF-OPENING

Pocket Diary

AND NOTE BOOK

for

1917,

containing coupon for

£1000 ACCIDENT INSURANCE

(For Details see Coupon).

Gold Medal and Diploma of Honour, Brussels Exh. 1907.

Diploma of Honour and Gold Medal, Franco-British Exh., 1908.

MR. JOHN LETTS
The First Diary Publisher.

Charles Letts & Co

LONDON.

(Copyright.)

Telephone No.: Hop Exchange 1250 (2 lines).

Telegraphic Address: "Diarists, London."

Amiel's tiny diary for 1917 measuring 5cm x 13cm when closed.

Extract from Amiel's Diary

Jan 1 Monday	Bank shut. Worked till 10pm.
Jan 2 Tuesday	Worked till 10.30pm.
Jan 3 Wednesday	Worked till 10.15pm.
Jan 4 Thursday	Worked till 10.45pm.
Jan 5 Friday	Worked till 10.30pm.
Jan 6 Saturday	Worked till 2pm. Went shopping with D. Bought hat shape. [D is her friend Dot Wayne].
Jan 7 Sunday	Father very bad. [ill] Quiet day. Rehearsal at Griffins for 3/4 hr.

7th Jan 1917
Newmarket

My dear Amiel,

It was really jolly good of you to sit up so late to write to me, you are a . . . (never mind what, but I will tell you when we meet again). I am so glad you liked the songs, I only wish I were able to be with you today to hear you sing them, but I mustn't think of such things as I shall only get fed up.

I will send you one or two more if I may. I wanted to do so yesterday but couldn't get into town in time, and I am afraid the selection in Newmarket is not a very good one. I will do my best though the next time I go down town.

Surely you know more about your voice than I do, so why ask me. I thought you sang toppingly and only hope I shall be able to hear you many <u>many</u> more times.

I had a fine time of last Thursday. Six of us gave a concert at a place near here to all the villagers and after the show we were entertained by Viscountess Annersley at her house. She invited a few of her friends and we made a party of about a dozen. We had fine grub and I quite felt a nib particularly when we had finger bowls after dinner, things I have never used before. She sent us home about 3am in her car. I do wish you could have seen me, I talked to the old girl as though I had mixed in court circles all my life and I hope I didn't make any terrible mistakes.

Miss Nock used to live next to some friends of mine in Church Hill Road, but I never met her, in fact I don't know her by sight. But still I trust she hasn't anything very awful to say about me.

I still live in hopes about the photo. If I had you with me here or if I were at Handsworth I shouldn't be so anxious as I should have <u>you</u>, at least I hope I should, but as I have to exist on the remembrance of those very few happy days together I hope your Mother will relent and send it along.

I must finish this off soon now as the post goes very early here on Sunday. I had a very exciting dream last night, that I had about an hour's leave between 1 and 2 and that I was trying to find you first at the Bank and then on the tram, but I never did find you so I decided to wake up.

Just write as soon as you can please. I shall be anxiously looking out for it, but I am looking forward mostly to the time when I can come and see you again. I wonder what will happen then, I think we had better wait and see don't you, because you never really know.

In your next letter will you please tell me the date of your birthday, as I am going to make up a yarn so that I can try to wangle a weekend off and it would be jolly nice if I could come on that date. I think you said it was early in February.

Give my kindest regards to all at home and my love to you.

Yours affectionately, Norman.

Can you find out how Percy Robinson is, and please give my best wishes to Jimmy D. How much does he know?

Extract from Amiel's Diary

Jan 8 Monday	Stayed in bed all day. Letter from N.
Jan 9 Tuesday	Stayed at the bank till 6pm.
Jan 10 Wednesday	Allies concert at Nineveh Road [Handsworth].
Jan 11 Thursday	Rehearsal put off.
Jan 12 Friday	Letter from N. Rehearsal. Late at bank.
Jan 13 Saturday	Miss Millnor's party. I felt very bad. Dot here for weekend.
Jan 14 Sunday	Lazy day. Dot helped make blue velvet hat. Letter from N.

11th Jan 1917
Newmarket

My dear Amiel,

I was so glad to get your letter this morning, it was good of you to write and you have no idea how I look forward to getting them, it is the next best thing now that I can't see you.

I am sorry the last songs were too low, but don't trouble to send them back as it isn't worth it as I doubt if I could get them in another key. I sent another song yesterday which I hope you will like, I thought it would suit you and I rather liked it.

As regards leave, I don't know when I shall come, I shall have to invent some awful yarn, but when I do you will have to spend every minute of the time with me, so I will not come on the 10th Feb if I can help it. You have no idea how much I want to see you again, perhaps the next time I come we can talk over many things.

I am awfully sorry to hear that you have been ill, you must get well soon and let me know how you are going along. I don't like to think you are ill, I feel so helpless being so far from you, but I know you will get every attention possible.

Would it be a terrible effort for you to write every other day, I should really be awfully bucked if you did, and I will do the same. So please do this, I am quite sure you will, as I am sure you understand how much I want to hear from you.

I do hope we get a chance to get a long while together before I go to France, as I should hate to go and leave you as we are now. I don't know your thoughts about things but I know mine, and I hope we shall think more of each other when I do go than we do now. This last sounds a strange sentence but you will understand me I know.

I shall write again on Saturday and every other day after that, so please do the same dear and I shall be very grateful.

With much love, Yours affectionately, Norman.
I still persist and am afraid I shall continue.

PS I hope your Mother and Father are quite well again now. What about that photo?????

Saturday, 13th Jan 1917
Newmarket

My dear Amiel,

I am writing to you today as I said I would in my last letter and hope you don't mind, but I don't suppose you do.

It is an absolutely rotten day here, all rain and snow and tons of mud about the camp, it is nothing but cleaning boots the whole day long. We had our first exam yesterday. I think I did fairly well but nothing extra, but better than several men. Today I feel I should just like to be at Holly Road with you, by the fire and to have some music, it seems ages since Xmas and since I saw you, although it really isn't so very long ago. There has been a further order out that no leave is to be allowed in any circumstances. It seems jolly hard lines, but I suppose it can't be helped and we must wait until I finish here in March, unless you can persuade your Mother or Mrs Easy to bring you down here for a weekend, but more of that later.

I went to see the *Battle of the Somme* in the pictures on Wednesday; it was very good but rather gruesome for relatives of men in the army, but I expect you have seen it yourself. I wish we could go to the pictures tonight, don't you?

Do you know a song called *Your Smile*, it is rather old but I am very keen on it and if you haven't got it let me know as I should very much like to hear you sing it.

I am hoping to get a letter tomorrow from you and every other day if you can manage it. I hope you are quite well again now, I am fairly fit, but have a rotten cold.

With much love, Yours affectionately, Norman.

[The Battle of the Somme was a documentary and propaganda silent film released in August 1916 and seen by 20 million – nearly half the population in Britain at this time. People could recognise their relatives and friends. You can watch it on YouTube.]

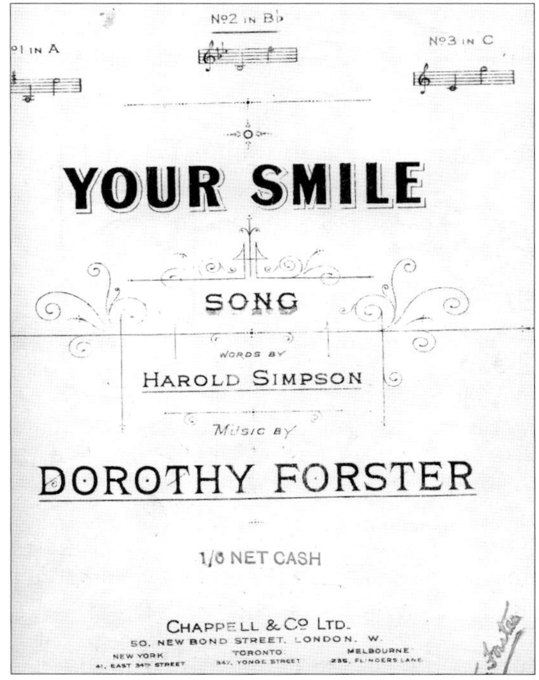

Sheet music for Your Smile.

16th Jan 1917
Newmarket

My dear Amiel,

Many thanks for your letter today, I had been expecting it before but I will forgive you as you say you didn't have a chance sooner.

You must excuse this letter being in pencil but I am sitting near the fire, it is so awfully cold in this hut.

I am glad you liked the song and am anxious to hear you sing it – I will send *Your Smile* as soon as I can but I am having to stay in camp all this week as I am in charge of the fire picquet. [fire watch duty] I will see you get it as soon as I go down town again.

You may be sure I shall not get fed up to having a letter every other day, as I told you before you are the only girl I write to, although you seem to imagine I am a terrible sort of person, but I am not really if you only knew me thoroughly. Just write to me as I suggested please unless of course you really object to do so so often, but I hope you don't. You can be quite sure I shall never get tired of having letters from you – news about yourself is what I want, not about other people.

I am very glad you are better; I am quite fit, except for this wretched cold which I think means to last for ever.

In reply to your query, I meant, did Mr D know how much we had seen of each other at Xmas, and your letters are not destroyed – strange n'est ce pas? [this may be Mr Davidson from the Bank, see letter of 2nd January.]

I won't ask for the photo again until I return home again, you don't seem to understand me a little bit; I don't think of you a bit like other girls, and even then I haven't known such a lot as you imagine.

I, like you, am sorry about the leave, but I shall get home again as soon as I can get passed out from here, which will be in March I expect, so let us look forward to that time, and what a time we will have. It is a great pity we didn't know each other before Xmas, but that can't be helped and we must make the best of writing letters.

I shall be looking out for another letter from you soon so please don't disappoint me.

I know you are not like the average modern girl – thank goodness, and that is why I think about you as I do – you don't know what I mean I know, but I will tell you someday perhaps, if you want me to.

With much love, Yours affectionately, Norman.
You see I still persist in my ending. I don't usually end letters like this, but I will to you if you don't mind.

Extract from Amiel's Diary

Jan 15 Monday	Mother & I went to *Yeomen of the Guard*.
Jan 16 Tuesday	Met Lois had tea Wedgwood. Copied O *Flower Divine*. [1915 song by Wood and Teschemacher].
Jan 17 Wednesday	Stayed late and sorted cheques. Letter from N.
Jan 18 Thursday	Miss Pilcher and I couldn't get in for the *Gondoliers*. Went to the Pictures.
Jan 19 Friday	Stayed at Bank late.
Jan 20 Saturday	Letter from N. Allies at Stourbridge. Dots Party. Fearful time in the con. Girls from Dots put up at Midland Hotel.
Jan 21 Sunday	Got up at 10. Lazy day. Music.

19th Jan 1917,
Newmarket

My dear Amiel,

I was very pleased to get your letter this morning and hope you will receive this during the weekend at Smethwick. [He may have meant Stourbridge, which is mentioned in Amiel's diary.]

I have never seen *The Yeomen* but should very much like to have been with you, I have heard how good it is, but *Iolanthe* will always be my favourite, I suppose it is perhaps because it was the first piece in which I played. I am afraid I was very feeble in it, but I should very much like to have another chance. I think though nowadays I am a bit too heavy to do Strephon, the sentry [son of Iolanthe] is more in my line.

I know a bit about the *Sorcerer* as I was once given a part in it, but couldn't play it for some reason. I don't think it is up to the usual standard.

It is a pity Mr Easy couldn't get into the Buffs. I am sure he would have had a better time than in any other regiment; I often think of the very happy days I had with the boys there.

I sang at a concert here on Wednesday and there is another tonight, Friday, but I haven't anything very special to sing so have gone back to some of my earliest numbers and think of giving *England* and *Stone Cracker John* and I have one or two little Irish songs I can do if required – which is not very likely.

The books by Kipling I liked were *Plain Tales from the Hills*, *More Plain Tales* and *Life's Destiny*. I think this latter is the title, or it is something like that. Don't blame me if they don't suit your tastes as they are hardly books for girls, but they are just what I like.

We have had a rotten day today in the trenches, mud up to our knees nearly and we didn't come out until it was quite dark. We were all very tired and glad to get back to a good feed.

I will write you again on Sunday and hope to hear from you very soon.

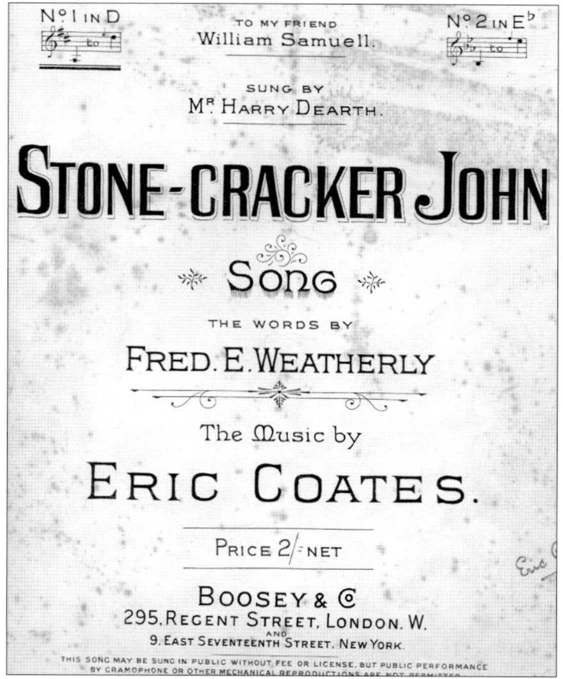

Sheet music for Stone Cracker John.

I hope the concert is a success on Saturday, just think of me when you are singing and I will send you a song as soon as I can get down town.

With much love, Yours affectionately, Norman.

Extract from Amiel's Diary

Jan 22 Monday	Came home. Letter from N. Dot slipped down going to the Bank.
Jan 23 Tuesday	In bed with influenza. M bought mimosa sweets. F bought oranges.
Jan 24 Wednesday	Called at Doctors. Not in. Felt bad but went to the Bank.
Jan 25 Thursday	Met F. He bought me birthday present, lovely bag. Notecase to match. Letter. Song *Any place is Heaven when you are near me.*
Jan 26 Friday	Wore Dot's pink jersey. Left Bank early. Went to Griffins. Bath. Bed.
Jan 27 Saturday	Stayed in bed all day. Madge called about skating. Ice not ready.
Jan 28 Sunday	Stayed in bed. Got up 6 o'clock. Wrote letters.
Jan 29 Monday	Allies at Sutton Coldfield. Cold too bad to go. Letter from N. Away from Bank.
Jan 30 Tuesday	Went to Bank. Cold very bad.
Jan 31 Wednesday	Late night. Letter from N.
Feb 1 Thursday	F's card friend here. T has bad cold. Away from office. [T unknown.].
Feb 2 Friday	Late at Bank. Called at Griffins. Called for F & M at Jim B's. Intro to his fiancée. Letter from N.
Feb 3 Saturday	Allies concert Churchfields, West Bromwich. Cold too bad to go. Sore throat. Skating with Lillie.
Feb 4 Sunday	Skating with Father. M went to see W. Warren. Rehearsal at 8 o'clock.

[Amiel's birthday is on 7th February so the presents from her father are perhaps a bit early. She's obviously struggling with flu but is conscientiously trying to go to work during the busiest period for balancing the books at the end of the month. But she's a bit naughty going ice skating in the cold with a sore throat! I haven't been able to work out who T refers to.

The song *Any place is Heaven when you are near me* was sung by John McCormack, an Irish tenor, who was the first artist to record the better known *It's a long way to Tipperary* in 1914.

There must be some letters missing but now lost, as there seems to be a gap between 19th and 31st January if Norman was writing every other day as he had promised.]

[*undated, but probably 31st Jan 1917 from Newmarket – first page is missing*]

. . . to imply that I thought you were cold, but you certainly are very cautious. Not that I mind, in fact I think heaps more of you for it, but when I come to you again I hope everything will be straightened out. I mustn't say too much must I? But I do want to see you again so that we can have a talk about things.

It is time for me to push off to the concert now. I shall be thinking of you and I only wish you could be there. Goodnight dearest, I will write more tomorrow.

Thursday
I will just finish off this letter today although there is not a lot to add.

We left here at 3.30 yesterday and went to a village called Soham, we were entertained to a fine tea and then gave the concert. I only sang two songs and one encore, but *Barnicombe Fair* didn't go down very well, so I shall cut it out in future. After the show we had a fine supper and met some very jolly people and got back here in fairly decent time. I understand they want us to go out there again in a week or two's time.

Every day that goes means a day nearer to seeing you and now that February is here I hope time soon goes. Write soon please and I should like a letter every other day if you can manage it.

With all my love, Yours affectionately, Norman.

3rd Feb 1917
Newmarket

My darling Amiel,

I do hope you had a nice time at the dance yesterday, or was it Friday, and don't I wish I could have come with you, but you might have objected as I should have wanted to have had all the dances with you. I wondered several times how you were getting on and whether you had met anyone there very nice. Anyway I hope there was no-one who will try to take you from me or there will be some bloodshed.

I went over to Fordham last night [4 miles north of Newmarket], had quite a good time. My friends motored me over and I sang two songs and two encores and people seemed to be very pleased. There was a dance after the concert, but as I am not a little bit keen on dancing I went to my friends' house which was quite near to the concert hall, and played billiards until a late hour. It is getting near the end of our course now, but the worst is we are having reveille [woken up by bugle call] at 6 o'clock in future, which to say the least is a bit rotten. It is much colder here now and to turn out at six makes me shiver to think of it.

I sent you a song yesterday which I hope you will like. I haven't heard any nice ones for ages; can you suggest any you would like me to send; don't be shy at asking because you know nothing gives me more pleasure, and besides all I have sent so far are just my own choice and not yours. Thank you very much for your letter this morning.

With all my love, Always your Norman.

Just another for you if you have been a good girl x
Do your Mother and Father think we are strange persons writing so much, or do they know the truth?

3rd Feb 1917, Newmarket
[This is the second letter for this date, presumably in answer to Amiel's letter received after Norman had written the letter above]

My dearest Amiel,

Many thanks for your letter, you didn't say how you are. I wish you would always remember to do so, particularly as you have got the flu. I do wish I could come over and see you, it does seem rotten it can't be managed but of course it is impossible at present, and it may not be until March, but as soon as that happy day arrives you will get a wire and then we shall be with each other again.

I am sending you just a little present to remind you of your birthday. I am not sending you exactly what I should have liked as I should like to give you that at a later date – if you want it, but I won't tell you what it is until I see you again.

The thing I am sending I hope you will like, it was very difficult to think what you would like as I knew it was no use writing to ask you, but still I hope it arrives safely.

We have had a fine day today; we went out on patrol work. I think you know I rank as a sergeant here, for some peculiar reason, so I was in charge of a platoon. We got our work done fairly quickly so I went off with a corporal and found a nice cottage where we had tea by a good fire and drew maps of the dispositions of our men. We got them all in about 4 o'clock and sent them home. I was supposed to have gone to a battalion concert tonight but I have a rotten cold so I thought I would get out of it and write to you instead. It is jolly nice to have you to write to, particularly as I know you like to hear from me. You know I look forward to your letters, more than you think.

There is plenty of skating round here but I haven't done any here as I have no skates and it is so long since I did any I hardly feel like giving an exhibition to the Newmarket natives.

Have you got *I Think*, it is a jolly pretty song and if you don't know it I will send it along in due course.

My pal here has his girl down here, he is jolly lucky and I do envy him and I hope that perhaps after I get gazetted things will have altered sufficiently to allow you to come up to see me occasionally. [The London Gazette published appointments to military posts.]

I am just off to bed now and I will finish off this letter and will post it in the morning. I am always dreaming I am back at home with you, let us hope it is a good omen. Goodnight dearest.

With much love, Always your Norman.

Extract from Amiel's Diary

Feb 5 Monday	Doctor here. Allies concert at Harborne. Bad in bed with tonsillitis. N sent me serviette ring.
Feb 6 Tuesday	Letter from N. Mrs Chirm sent hankies.
Feb 7 Wednesday	Letter from N. Birthday. Heaps of presents. Doctor O'Dowd came.
Feb 8 Thursday	Letter from N. Sat up in my bedroom for a short time. Heating. Lillie called.
Feb 9 Friday	Sat up after dinner. Mrs Baker called.
Feb 10 Saturday	Allies concert at Knowle. Bad in bed still. Letter from N. Father's card friends here.
Feb 11 Sunday	Song from N. Came downstairs for first time. Sang *I Think*.

5th Feb 1917
Newmarket

My dearest Amiel,

You must excuse me writing this letter in pencil please but it is so much cosier to sit near the fire than to be away at the table.

You don't seem to mind at the way I started my letter so I will continue to do so. I don't see why I shouldn't write in that strain if I really mean it and if it is the truth it isn't silly is it? As regards meaning what I say, whatever I have said or written to you I have really honestly meant so please don't be horrid dear and say or imagine rotten things. If you do want me to say more than I intended, I will tell you I feel very differently towards you than I have ever felt to any other girl I have met, even including the girl to whom I was once engaged, and that is the truth and I hope you will believe what I say. It is so very hard to explain all these things in a letter and you must forgive me if I am not very clear, it is such a pity I can't come home to you we could soon settle things then. Never mind dear, I shall see you in another six weeks I hope, and six Sundays will soon rush by.

I am sorry to hear you have a sore throat, you have been very unfortunate lately and I do hope you will soon be better.

I must go now as I want this letter to get away tonight. You mustn't mind it being rather short but I will send more next time.

Give my kindest regards to your Mother and Father.
With much love, Yours affectionately, Norman.

6th Feb 1917
Newmarket

My dearest Amiel,

When your letter arrived I didn't know from whom it was, as I didn't recognise the writing on the envelope. I am so sorry to hear you have tonsillitis. I have never had it myself but I know it is a jolly rotten thing and I do hope you will soon be better. I shall write to you often while you are ill because I know how much I appreciate letters when I am ill. And another thing, you will want something to do during the day, so look how many letters you can write to me, six a day if you will, and you know how much I look out for them.

I am glad you liked the present, I wish I could be with you tomorrow as it is your birthday and then I could cheer you up and we could be happier being together, even if you are ill, than we are being so far off.

Is the girl in your troupe who has just got engaged anyone I know? I think it is about time someone else in your troupe thought about the same thing but I won't tell you her name, she must find out for herself.

It is most awfully cold here, even the vinegar and mustard on the table were frozen today so you can tell it is fairly chilly, but the sun is extra and I should just like a nice walk with you this afternoon and have tea out in the country somewhere.

As I wrote to you yesterday I am afraid I haven't so very much to say to you, but I will write again tomorrow if I can find time and I expect I shall be able to do so.

Be sure you let me know how your throat is and remember me to your Mother and Father please. It won't be so very long for us now; time soon goes.

With much love, Yours affectionately, Norman.

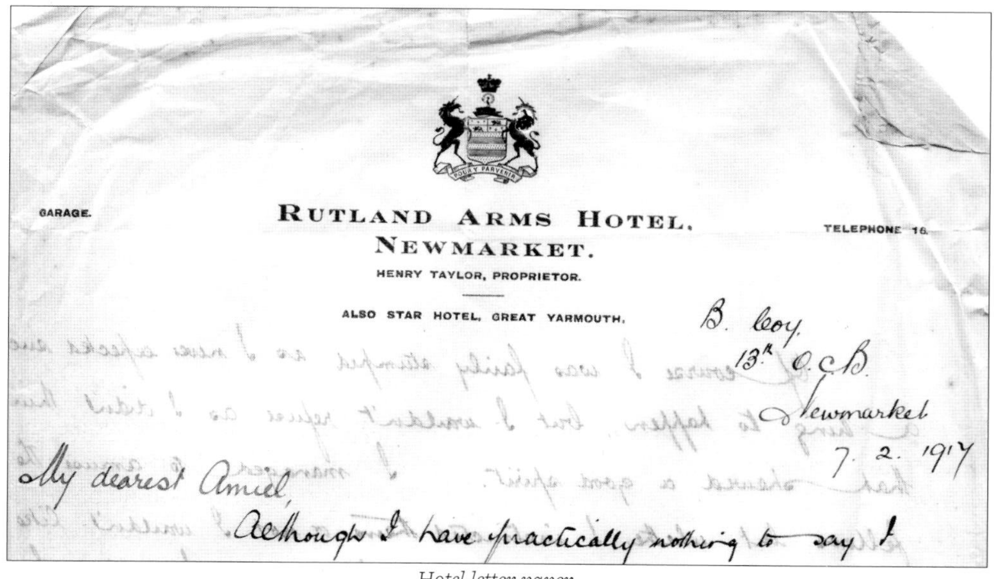

GARAGE.

RUTLAND ARMS HOTEL,
NEWMARKET.

HENRY TAYLOR, PROPRIETOR.

ALSO STAR HOTEL, GREAT YARMOUTH.

TELEPHONE 16.

B. Coy.
13th O.C.B.
Newmarket
7. 2. 1917

My dearest Amiel,

Although I have practically nothing to say I

Hotel letter paper.

7th Feb 1917
Newmarket

My dearest Amiel,

Although I have practically nothing to say I thought I would just send a line to cheer you up if possible, while you are in bed. Isn't it jolly cold, but I suppose you are nice and cosy in bed. I am sure it is the best place in this weather, but unfortunately we have to turn out at 6.30 and I think the most awful sound on these mornings is reveille. If we don't get up immediately and rush about fairly quickly we can't get ready for our parade at 7.30.

Last night I had a fearful ordeal. An officer was to have lectured to us but he couldn't do so, so I was called up out of the audience to lecture on anything.

Of course I was fairly stumped as I never expected such a thing to happen, but I wouldn't refuse as I didn't think that showed a good spirit. I managed to amuse the fellows but whether I instructed them or not I wouldn't like to say. Anyway the O.C. was very pleased so I suppose I must expect a repetition fairly soon.

I have just fed at this hotel, hence the pretty paper, and I am just going to the Pictures with some fellows. Don't I wish you could come with me, it would be heaps nicer for both of us, wouldn't it. Please write soon.

With very much love, Yours affectionately, Norman.

9th Feb 1917
Newmarket

My dearest Amiel,

Very many thanks for your letter, you don't know how welcome it was as I was feeling so very fed up. I have a touch of the flu I think. It is very good of you to write down your thoughts as you do, I do appreciate it. I often feel like expressing all mine to you but don't know whether I ought as you may not think it right seeing what a short time we had together at Xmas. Never mind, I shall soon be coming home now I hope and then all will be different for we shall then know how we stand. You are jolly lucky to be at home, it makes me very envious and I almost wish I were a girl sometimes, as this war seems to upset everything. I don't think you a bit mad by telling me the things you do and I only hope on your next birthday I shall be able to give a big hug and a kiss as your mother did on this one. Don't think me very cheeky for saying this dear will you, I am only saying what I really mean and think.

Fancy, you are now twenty, and you are wondering whether the next twenty years will be as happy as the last. Well dearest I do hope they will and I only hope I shall be able to help to make them happy. You must think I am a strange person saying the things I do to you, but it is much better to be honest and I am sure I have never written such things to any other girl although you seem to say you imagine I am a terrible sort of youth.

We are going to Brandon on Monday for five days, so please send letters to N.A.W. 13th Officers Cadet Battn., c/o Post Office, Brandon, Suffolk. We shall be leaving there on the Friday so you must judge when to cease sending them there.

Goodnight dearest; when next you write tell me how you are. Give my kindest regards to your Mother and Father.

With all my love, Yours affectionately, Norman.
Haven't you a little bit of love to spare for me?

11th Feb 1917
Newmarket

My dearest Amiel,

You are a lucky girl to have had such a heap of presents for your birthday. I expect I shall spend mine in a dugout in France, thinking of you at home and wishing I could be with you.

I am not looking forward to my next leave except for seeing you as I am sure Mother will be very upset. She knows it will be my last leave at home. When I have gone to France you will have to go round to my home and cheer her up, because I am hoping you will come round and meet my folks next month. It isn't much more than 4 or 5 weeks now so we can start looking forward to it.

I sent you a song last night and hope you will like it. I thought it sounded rather nice and I am hoping to hear you sing it soon.

I hope you are better now. I am pleased to say I am feeling much better and I hope with care to be quite well by tomorrow. It is so rotten in the army when you are not well as there is very little comfort here; but I have been very careful and having heaps of Bovril which has done wonders.

As you know we are off to Brandon in the morning and I will send my address as soon as I get there. I am afraid this isn't a very interesting letter and not very long, but I want to catch the post and I have to pack up all my kit. Please write soon, and let me know if you are better.

With much love, Yours affectionately, Norman.

Extract from Amiel's Diary

Feb 12 Monday	Letter from N. F & Mother went skating. Doctor called.
Feb 13 Tuesday	Letter from N. Mrs Baker came in for the afternoon. Jim called with books.
Feb 14 Wednesday	Letter from N. Waynes came. Dot stayed the night. Talked till 3 o'clock.
Feb 15 Thursday	Letter from N. M and I went a little walk. Bought camisole material. Lois came. Tea. Music.
Feb 16 Friday	Bed till dinner time. Made camisole. F went to cards.
Feb 17 Saturday	Allies concert at Whittaker [This must be Whitacre, Coleshill.] Couldn't go. Cards all afternoon. Bed early.
Feb 18 Sunday	Stayed in. M went to Rednal Hospital. Went to Griffins at 3.30. Letter from Norman.

[Rednal Hospital, or Rubery Hospital at Rednal, formerly an asylum, was taken over by the military and used for war casualties, becoming the first Birmingham War Hospital. Other military hospitals in Birmingham included Monyhull in King's Norton, Birmingham University – which became the First Southern General Hospital, Poor Law Infirmary in Dudley Road, school buildings in King's Heath, and Stirchley, Rubery Hill and Hollymoor hospitals were also used. Auxiliary hospitals or convalescent homes were also created in some of the larger houses such as Highbury in Moseley, Moor Green Hall, Harborne Hall, The Beeches in Erdington, Uffculme, and Allerton in Sutton Coldfield. Many of these are mentioned in Amiel's diary as concert venues for 'The Allies' troupe.]

12th Feb 1917 [written on a printed Letter Card, with preprinted stamp]
The Ram Hotel
Brandon
Suffolk

My dearest Amiel,

I thought I would let you know I am here safely in a topping billet. We shall be here until Friday as you know so you had better not write here after Wednesday but to the usual address at Newmarket. I will write a letter tomorrow.
Much love, Norman.

13th Feb 1917
The Ram Hotel
Brandon

My dearest Amiel,

Your letter today was very welcome, it was nice to hear from you in this place as we seem so far from everyone. It is an awfully pretty town and it must be very nice in the summer, but at present there is plenty of snow about although it is not really so cold.

Our billet here is awfully comfortable, it is quite a treat to be in a decent bed again and we have a most cosy sitting room all to ourselves. I am very tired this evening as we have had a long day but I thought I would write this as I like to sit down and have a talk with you when I can.

As regards telling you my thoughts dearest, you can surely almost guess what they are as regards you, and I shall soon be home now and will tell you everything. We are going to have a real good time together as it may be our last for some time. I never think anything will happen to me in the fighting and the war can't last for ever so I shall be with you for good then. As to telling you what I told Mother at Xmas, I am afraid you will have to wait, I really couldn't put it on paper but you shall hear all in good time.

I am looking forward to your next birthday for reasons which you know, but strange things may happen before then so I may not have to wait quite as long as that. Thank you for the very small portion of love, it may grow great in time – I do hope so.

With much love, Yours affectionately, Norman.

14th Feb 1917
Brandon

My dearest Amiel,

I am afraid this will only be a short letter tonight as I am feeling jolly tired, but I don't like going to bed without sending you a few lines even if it is only very few. It was very kind of you to write again so soon, I really feel dear we are getting to know each other's feelings now and it is heaps better. I am feeling a lot better now thank you and in a day or two I shall be quite fit although last week I was about as miserable as I could be. As you say I am hoping to get a fairly long leave and we will spend every available minute together if you are willing. As regards my Mother, when I am in France nothing will be more cheering to her than to have someone with her whom she knows I am fond of, and I am certain she will like you very much and you will like her I know. I can take you round to my home as soon as I get back there.

Why are you so afraid your writing so often to me will be considered foolish and forward? Surely you know me sufficiently dearest to do away with all such thoughts as those. If I don't write to you every day you know it is only because I haven't the opportunity and so I expect you to write just whenever you can. What other people would say shouldn't affect us in the least.

I am glad you like the song, I do very much.

Don't end your letters in German again as I can't understand it and it isn't half so nice as English. It wouldn't take me more than three words to say what I think of you and I think English can express them best. You must wait though to know what those words are. I must finish off now so goodnight dearest and I should like to give you what is promised for next birthday – really.

With much love, Yours affectionately, Norman.
Albert – rotten isn't it? [*Amiel must have asked what his middle initial A stood for*]

16th Feb 1917
Newmarket

My dearest Amiel,

You really are an angel to write to me so that I had your letter when I got back to Newmarket. I am feeling very tired after a long day and a long march and am off to bed in two seconds, but I want to end the day with just a few words to you.

We had a fine time at Brandon, we were there on a course of firing and field manoeuvres and being in such a topping billet it made even our hard work quite a nice change and we are all rather sorry to be back in these draughty old huts again.

I am glad you are getting better, do be very careful and don't get a return of the flu.

As regards sending you a pattern letter, aren't you rather one of those people who have eyes and see not? Surely dearest you must have discovered that by this time we are getting just a little more than friends, at least I hope so, and I should like to feel you think that way. It is very hard for us I know, being so far apart, but it is rather nice if we don't keep in the usual conventional way of letter writing and that is why I begin and end my letters as I do. I like to call you 'dearest' because you are, as regards my love, you ought to know by now you have it all and so I send it. I have put now just what my thoughts are and that is what you asked for, and it is quite the truth so I do hope you won't think it foolish and frivolous because it is not meant to be.

I hope you get this letter when you are feeling serious because I am quite serious in what I have put, and I do hope I see you soon.

Try and think of me as one who is very fond of you and who knows you better than you think.

Goodnight darling and don't think me foolish will you?
With much love, Always your Norman.

18th Feb 1917
Newmarket

My dearest Amiel,

I am afraid my last one or two letters have been rather irregular but of course with moving from Brandon it has rather upset our spare time.

I am enclosing the photo. I don't like it at all but it was very cheap and it was taken on my first walk after getting out of bed from the flu. [photo not in archive]

The fellow with me is my chief pal, named Shaw, and one of the very best, although it is not very good of him.

You have no idea how much mud we have here, it is about a foot deep all over the camp and I seem to do nothing but clean my boots all day long.

Yesterday I spent the afternoon at some friends in the country and had a very nice time but often thought of you and wished you could have been there. I sang, played a bit and then played billiards and got back here about 9 o'clock.

In about a month from now I hope to be with you again and I am looking forward to seeing you. I often lie in bed and think what fine times we will have and what we will do and I only hope it will come off.

Now you have been ill don't you think you might persuade your Mother to bring you down here for a few days? It is quite a nice place and there are several good houses where you could stay and it would be jolly nice for both of us. Try and do your best will you dear?

Did I tell you we had a gramophone in our hut, it is just playing 'The Languid Melody' from 'The Bing Boys', it is topping and makes me wish I had you here with me. I should so like to take you out for the day. Please write soon.

With all my love, Always your Norman.

[*The Bing Boys are Here Again* was a series of revues, opening in 1916 and included the famous song *If You Were the Only Girl in the World,* and *Yula Hicki Wicki Yacki Dula*. It was one of the three most important musicals during WW1, the others being *Chu Chin Chow* and *The Maid of the Mountain* – see Amiel's diary entry for 13th March.]

19th Feb 1917
Newmarket

My dearest Amiel,

Very many thanks for your letter this morning, I am glad you are gradually getting better and hope by the time I come home again you will be quite well and able to be with me all the time. There is another rumour about leave but I am afraid there is no truth in it, but our final exam is to be about March 21st and I shall be soon with you after this date, in fact I hope in five weeks from now I shall be with you by a nice fire in a cosy armchair (singular not plural) either at your house or mine.

It is to be hoped there will be some decent things on at the theatres when I get back so that we can go together.

Now dearest, I want to ask you to do something for me. When you are well enough will you have a small photo of yourself taken so that I can have it in a case to take to France with me? I shall want cheering up when I am in my dugout and it will be jolly nice to have a photo of you to look at. I am just off to bed and will finish this in the morning so goodnight dearest.

Tuesday
I haven't much to add to this letter, I want to get it away soon so that you will get it tomorrow and I hope to hear from you soon. Do you know *Tired Hands*, it is one of my favourites and you may like it if you haven't got it. You must tell me if you don't like the style of songs I send you and I will send some different ones. Don't forget about having your photo taken and please write soon. I shall soon be with you now and I am counting up the days.

With much love, Yours affectionately, Norman
Did that one letter of yours use up all the love you can spare? I wish you weren't so cautious, surely you know me by now.

Extract from Amiel's Diary

Feb 19 Monday	Stayed in washed head. Mrs Masters came. F went to opera *Aida*. Letter and photo.
Feb 20 Tuesday	Waited for Doctor all day. Rehearsal at night.
Feb 21 Wednesday	Called at Mrs Appleby's. Went to Weaver's. Letter from Norman.
Feb 22 Thursday	Went to the Bank after 2 weeks & 4 days away.
Feb 23 Friday	Letter from N. Allies Concert at St Francis. [A social centre and church in Handsworth.] Went off splendidly. Dot W stayed the night. All went to Griffins afterwards.
Feb 24 Saturday	Mr Sargeant's and Miss Strauche's wedding. Taxied there & after the ceremony went to the house. Letter from N.
Feb 25 Sunday	Letter from N. I went to James. Lillie and Louie there. Topping time.
Feb 26 Monday	Allies Concert. Monyhull, King's Norton. [Monyhull military hospital – saw several thousand wounded and shell shocked soldiers in WW1.] Gwen Cattell & Ethel Hill away. Got on all right. N. Hill came.
Feb 27 Tuesday	Allies Concert, Saltley [east of Birmingham city centre.] V. Osborne and N. Hill came. Very enthusiastic.
Feb 28 Wednesday	Letter from N. Singing lesson. Was at Dale Fortys. [Dale, Forty & Co was a piano company.] M & F at Wayne's. Letter from N.

The Allies *in costume. Amiel is in the Flag outfit.*
Back row L-R: Madge Griffin, Amiel Robins, Edie Durban.
Seated L-R: Gwen Cattell, Mr Griffin, Dorothy Durban.
Front row L-R: Ethel Hill, Beryl Stokes, Gladys Marson.

Extract from Amiel's Diary

Mar 1 Thursday	Letter from N.
Mar 2 Friday	Fancy dress at St Francis Institute. Allies went in their costumes.
Mar 3 Saturday	Allies at Coleshill. Slept till 4. Letter from N.
Mar 4 Sunday	Song *Tired Hands* from N. F & I went to see Mr Warren and Brett at Rubery.
Mar 5 Monday	Madge & I went to Mrs Peckhams at 7 to try songs out. Mr Griffin at Rhos.
Mar 6 Tuesday	Letter from N. Father at Mr Hollis's. M came to bed with me.
Mar 7 Wednesday	Letter from N. Mr Peckham's concert. Madge & I did several turns. Had tea with M in town.
Mar 8 Thursday	Mr Wilson came into Bank. I went to the Grand to see Margaret Cooper. Mrs W came late. [Margaret Cooper, singer & pianist. She was very highly paid for the time and popular with audiences, combining humour with musical composition.].

Mar 9 Friday	Heavy fall of snow. Couldn't go to the theatre. Came home & sang.
Mar 10 Saturday	Letter from N. M & I went about photos to U.S.A. Followed F to Mr Robinson's. Jolly evening with them. Mrs R knew Norman well.
Mar 11 Sunday	F & I went to Rednal Hosp; Called at Wilson's coming home. Vaughtons there.
Mar 12 Monday	Letter from N. Allies at Churchfields, W. Bromwich. Photo of N outside hut.

[Vaughtons, established 1819, are still manufacturers of handmade insignia (car badges, chains of office etc) in Birmingham's Jewellery Quarter. The family was well known in Handsworth.]

Norman outside his hut in Newmarket.

Norman and others.

Extract from Amiel's Diary

Mar 13 Tuesday	M & I went to *The Maid from the Mountains*, topping. Called about photos.
Mar 14 Wednesday	Letter from N. Aubrey Guest came home on leave. Misses Hodgkins and Griffiths to tea.
Mar 15 Thursday	Allies Y.M.C.A. Dale End. Last show for sometime. Everybody bad.
Mar 16 Friday	Letter from N. Had singing lesson at Dale Forty's.
Mar 17 Saturday	Letter from N. Card men here all afternoon.
Mar 18 Sunday	F & I went to Old Handsworth Church. Quiet day at home. Finished hat for Mrs Hollis. F & M went to Hurley Robinsons.

[Archibald Hurley Robinson was a prolific architect in Birmingham known for his pre WWII cinemas and later office buildings in the Midlands. In an autograph album of Amiel's he drew a beautiful pen and ink sketch of a house with gate pillars carved with Wandsworth [sic] House.]

Friday [probably 16th March]
Newmarket

My dearest Amiel,

Many thanks for your letter this morning, I am still free from measles but I mustn't say too much, we are not yet out of danger and I shall not feel safe until I am in the train coming home to you.

You do say some unkind things in your letters, just fancy asking whether I really wanted you at home when I come. It makes me almost feel as if you want to be away, and of course if you would rather do that I don't want you to upset your arrangements. But I do wish you would believe me when I say I want to have you the whole time with me, I don't usually write a lot of things just to fill up the paper and you don't know how your saying things like that hurt. I know it is very difficult to express things clearly in letters but I have always tried to put down the truth and so why be so disbelieving? I am sure you didn't mean to hurt my feelings dearest, so you are quite forgiven, but in future do try to understand that I do want you, and to come home to find you gone away would upset me very much. I don't want you to alter your arrangements on my account but you know what I want don't you?

With luck, a fortnight today I hope to be on the way home and I do hope I shall know that you will be waiting for me, on the station if possible, and what a fine time we shall have to look forward to, if you are on your holidays starting the 3rd.

We have been out for the day on a fine scheme and we are just back tired and sleepy so I won't write any more just now, but of course will do so tomorrow or Sunday. Just do what you think best about my leave you know now what I want. Don't think I am grubby in what I have written but you really ought to know me by this time.

With all my love, Always your own, Norman.

20th March 1917
Newmarket

My dearest Amiel,

I was very pleased to get your letter today. As I had one yesterday it came as a very nice surprise. I am sorry if I always seem complaining about not getting letters, as a matter of fact you are really very good to write as much as you do, but it is such a treat to get them, I miss them if they should happen to be a day late.

The official date that we finish here is the 31st inst, that is Saturday week and there are only two things that might upset it viz:

1. Measles.
2. Failure in the exams.

I live in great hopes of being able to avoid both of these so don't forget the date and think of the Sunday after when I hope we shall have our first day together.

I do wish I could have been home to have seen *The Bing Boys*, I have wanted to see it for ages and have never had the chance; I expect you enjoyed it. I have never seen *Daddy Long Legs* so if it is in B'ham when we are there we will go most certainly.

Mr Spencer was in the Buffs with me and I knew him quite well, but he came to your office to take my place. I was on Securities and when I went to Hereford on the same job there he took my job at Bennetts Hill.

Mr Price's son is down here in the 12th Officer Cadet Battalion which adjoins our camp. He has been here about 2 months but I only met him last Saturday and very surprised I was to see him as we were at school together. [Mr Price works at the Bank.]

We have had a long day's marching and chasing about the country and just feel nice and tired. I just wish I could sit by the fire with you tonight, but that time will soon be here I hope.

With all my love, Always your own, Norman.

22nd March 1917
Newmarket

My dearest Amiel,

I was very much afraid I shouldn't be able to write you today as we have had a very busy time. They mean to work us hard until the last day here. We are still avoiding the measles alright and I hope all will go well until Saturday week when the great day comes. You can't tell how excited I begin to feel about it, it seems such a fearful time since I was with you that I can hardly believe I am to see you so soon. I keep feeling that something rotten will turn up in the meantime to upset our plans but let us live in hopes.

We are on an all night game tonight, so when you are nice and warm in bed I shall be crawling over ploughed fields in the dark. I am looking after the Verey lights; they are what we send up when we think the enemy are about and they have a very bright light like a large rocket. We are to stop an attack on Newmarket by another company and have to stop them about 3 miles from here. If you were coming with me it wouldn't be so bad as we could easily dodge off in the dark and have a quiet walk on our own.

I expect next week we shall have a very easy time particularly after the exam and it seems a pity that I can't get home until Saturday, but it can't be done. Anyway it won't be long now until I am home, this time next week I shall know my fate in the exam and also re measles. Just mind you keep free from colds and very fit so that we can have a good old time together. You can't tell how much I want to see you again dearest.

With all my love, Always your own Norman.
I am enclosing another photo of our hut and the inmates thereof.
[Not found in archive.]

Extract from Amiel's Diary

Mar 19 Monday	P.P.C. & letter from N. M, F & Peckhams & I saw *Bing Boys are Here.* Rubbish.
Mar 20 Tuesday	
Mar 21 Wednesday	Letter from N.
Mar 22 Thursday	M & I had a Turkish bath. [These were probably the public baths in Grove Lane, Handsworth, which opened in 1907.] Lewis F & friend came in for bridge.

Mar 23 Friday	Letter from N. F & I went to Mrs Chirm's. Mr C came here. Had lesson when I came back.
Mar 24 Saturday	Walked to Aston with bicycle. Tram back. Peckhams came for billiards.
Mar 25 Sunday	Letter from N. M goes to Rednal. Powell plays billiards.

23rd March 1917
Newmarket

My dearest Amiel,

I was very pleased to get your letter today, I hope we shall not have to write many more now as time is rolling on. I hope we don't seem very different to each other, as you seem to think we shall; I have very pleasant recollections of you at Xmas which I hope won't have altered by when I return although certainly our feelings towards each other are different. At least we did not express our feelings then while when next we meet we shall not be so shy after all these letters.

I am surprised to hear you didn't care for *The Bing Boys* I have always had such good accounts of it from people who have seen it in London, but perhaps it was a poor company you saw. I wonder if the quartet you heard are as good, as the one we put on here is really fine; I am <u>not</u> in it needless to say.

We are having a farewell concert here on Monday and we have some topping new items to put on. I am singing my old favourite *The Mountains of Mourne* with some new topical verses written by a fellow here and we have some fine concerted items.

We have had no further cases of measles and we hope we are nearly clear of all danger now. I expect next week I shall have a very rowdy time as we have a concert Monday and farewell dinners all the rest of the week, so I expect when you see me I shall have a pale face from late hours and high living.

It is most awfully cold again here and I shall be glad to get home if only to live in a house again for a few days. It seems ages since I was home and years since I saw you.

I am just off out to dinner at my friend's house, I wish you were going too.

With all my love, Always your Norman.
My, shan't we be excited this time next week?

26th March 1917
Newmarket

My dearest Amiel,

Very many thanks for your letter today which cheered me up muchly. Today is the eve of the great battle in the exam; I must say I haven't done any work today I haven't felt a bit like it. I cut myself a little while ago with my razor on the cheek and it caused a sceptic [sic] abscess which got rather painful so I went to the doctor's and he politely informed me that he would have to cut it out. This sounded cheerful but I told him to carry on and I had a very lively few minutes. I have just returned and feel very hungry as I bled like blazes and am all patched up. I shall look very pretty tonight at our concert as of course I am going to sing, but what the audience will think at my dial I don't know.

I do wish you were coming tonight, it would just make all the difference.

As regards what you say about everything going wrong nowadays, I often feel very tempted to think as you do but although I am not a bit of a religious chap I think I can say I do still keep my faith. It will all come right dearest I am quite certain, we are unable to see everything; remember we are not expected to know everything, and if we are only patient and trust in our old beliefs we shall come through alright.

Wish me luck for tomorrow. With all my love, Always your Norman.

What I look like now!!

28th March 1917
Newmarket

My dearest Amiel,

I haven't had a letter yet today but am hoping to get one tomorrow or perhaps second post today.

We had the great exam yesterday and I must say it was rather difficult, much harder than the last one, but I am of course hoping for the best and feel fairly confident. In fact I did my best and therefore couldn't do more, so if I have failed, I've failed and that is the end of it, but cheer up I'm very hopeful.

We have had a very lively time since the exam, a dinner last night and we went to bed at one o'clock. I felt very much inclined to stay in bed all morning I felt so sleepy, but I was so fearfully hungry I had to get up to breakfast at 8 as I couldn't prevail on any kind person to bring it to bed to me.

This morning we had a fancy dress parade, two of the fellows made up as fine girls and I wore my pyjamas and a kilt; we marched all round our own lines and then went over to the 12th O.C.B. lines much to their delight of course. We afterwards played the officers at football and managed to beat them.

If all is right with the exam I shall leave here on Saturday morning and hope to arrive at New St. [Birmingham New Street Station] Saturday afternoon. Perhaps you would like to meet me and we can have tea in town before I go home; I shall of course want to see you in the evening as well but shall have to take my kit home and see my folks for an hour or so.

I will wire you as soon as the results are out, which will probably be tomorrow, Thursday, and also will find out and let you know what time the train arrives. You haven't told me what you have done about your holidays, I hope you have freed them up alright and what a time we'll have, I'm getting awfully excited.

With much love, Always your Norman.

Extract from Amiel's Diary

Mar 26 Monday	P.P.C. from N. I go on 'Country & DCA'. [This is something to do with the Bank but I don't know what it means.] M & I go to dressmakers. F & M spend evening with Clark.
Mar 27 Tuesday	Letter from N.
Mar 28 Wednesday	
Mar 29 Thursday	Letter from N. M & I went to the Turkish Baths.
Mar 30 Friday	
Mar 31 Saturday	F read N's letter through the phone. Came home. N came 8 o'clock. Suffering from Septic poisoning.

30th March 1917
Newmarket

My dearest Amiel,

Many thanks for your letter. You will be pleased to hear I came out second in the exam, out of 150.

Never mind about your holidays, I hope to have some time with you after Easter.

As regards Sunday thank you very much for asking me but I am afraid my folks will want me home to dinner but I should like to come to tea if that is convenient to you.

I can't find out anything about my train, but hope to get home in the afternoon. As it is so uncertain about the time of arrival, don't come to the station, but I will come round to your house as soon after tea as possible, it will probably be about 6.30

Hoping to see you then.
With much love, Norman.

Extract from Amiel's Diary

Apr 1 Sunday	[Palm Sunday] Mrs Warren, Brett & Gina came. Splendid time. N came stayed till 9. We went to Mr & Mrs Fanners.
Apr 2 Monday	N came into Bank also Flo Edwards. They met me at 4. Villa Cross pictures. Intro to Mr & Mrs Wells. [Villa Cross was a picture house or cinema].
Apr 3 Tuesday	*Peg o' my Heart* with N & Mrs Wells. Topping. [This was a comedy by Hartley J. Manners.] Left Mrs W at P.O. in town.
Apr 4 Wednesday	[With heart shape pencilled over the 4] Met N 4 o'clock. Came up to tea. F at Abergavenny. Music!
Apr 5 Thursday	[Maundy Thu] Late at Bank. N helped. Tea at Oak Room. Evening at Mrs Wells. N took me to Mr & Mrs Fanners for F & M.
Apr 6 Friday	[Good Friday] Glorious day. Walked to Sutton Park. Dinner at Royal Hotel. Tea at Mrs Wells. Music etc.
Apr 7 Saturday	Town with M & N. Bought mac. Met Mrs Warren, Brett etc. Went to Mr Hares with N. Lovely time.
Apr 8 Sunday	[Easter Sunday] Got breakfast. N & I went to Old Handsworth Church. Music. Quiet evening at home.
Apr 9 Monday	N & I went walk. Met M & F coming from Fanners. Snowstorm. Tea at Mrs W. Called at Mrs Fanners. Mrs F gave me *Maid of the Mountains.*
Apr 10 Tuesday	Went to town. Bank crowded. Went to Masonic tea at Mrs Wells.
Apr 11 Wednesday	N & I went walk to Uplands. N, M & I went to Mrs Bennewith. Went round to Palethorpes. [A company of that name which specialised in cooked meat and pastry products, especially sausages, began in Birmingham in the 1850s but this may be an unconnected family.] Home 10pm. Terrific snowstorm.
Apr 12 Thursday	Went to town for tickets. Went to pictures. Tea at Mrs Wells. Repertory Theatre – *Merry Wives of Windsor*. [Opened in 1913 as Britain's first purpose-built repertory theatre, and still exists in Station Street, now known as the Old Rep.]
Apr 13 Friday	N & I went to Sutton. My ankle was painful. Lunch at Royal Hotel [Sutton Coldfield] Walked to bus.
Apr 14 Saturday	Went to town.
Apr 15 Sunday	Went walk. Met Mr Wells. N & I went to Sutton. Walked round Blackroot Pool. [This is in Sutton Park.] Tea at Royal Hotel. Walked to bus.

Apr 16 Monday	Frank died 1 year ago. We tried to see *Milestones*. Crowded. Went to Masonic Hall. Tea with Mrs Wells. Quiet evening.
Apr 17 Tuesday	We went to Stonebridge. Had lunch. Walked on to Hampton in Arden. I said yes then turned round again. [Norman in his letter of 6th May mentions Berkswell which is near to Hampton in Arden].
Apr 18 Wednesday	Went to town. Called at the Bank. N bought some of his kit.
Apr 19 Thursday	N went to Masons to sit for his photo. Saw Martin Harvey in *David Garrick*. Splendid. [Sir John Martin-Harvey became an actor-manager].

[I had no idea who Frank was until I discovered some photographs with Frank B. B. pencilled on the reverse. One photograph is of Frank before he went off to train in Wensley, Yorkshire, and is dated 16th July 1915. Frank B. Brettell, who was from Handsworth, died aged 22 in France and is buried at Etaples Military Cemetery. He was a Lance Corporal in the Royal Warwickshire Regiment (14th Bn). I don't know how Amiel knew him or how well.]

Norman as 2nd Lieutenant.

Extract from Amiel's Diary

Apr 20 Friday	Tram to Yardley. Bus to Stonebridge. Walk to Meriden. N decides not to go away. Tea at Mrs Wells
Apr 21 Saturday	Went to town. *There's a Ship that's bound for Blighty*. [I assume she bought the song sheet.] Started on Botanical Gardens. Went to *Milestones*. Splendid. F out. M in to tea. Music. Went walk. Answered N's ? yes. [sic] [This was possibly Norman asking Amiel if she would marry him. The exchange of rings and official engagement didn't come till later. See May 26th.].
Apr 22 Sunday	Went a walk. Dinner. Started for Sutton [Coldfield]. Went to Botanical Gardens. Came home. Went into Park. F & M went to Mrs Wilson.
Apr 23 Monday	I went back to Bank. Had lunch with N at Pattersons. [sic – Pattisons Restaurant was just off Corporation Street in the city centre.] Met N at 4 & went to his home. Quiet time. Walk round the allotments.
Apr 24 Tuesday	I develop German Measles. Doctor comes. N goes as 2nd Lieut. of 1st Herefords to Oswestry.
Apr 25 Wednesday	Bad in bed. 2 Letters from N.
Apr 26 Thursday	Eyes bad nasty, dark room all day long.
Apr 27 Friday	Still bad.
Apr 28 Saturday	Awful pains all day. Doctor came 11.30pm
Apr 29 Sunday	Letter from N. F went to Coventry to see U. Fred. Felt better.
Apr 30 Monday	Letter from N also regimental ribbon & badge. Mrs Wells called, also 9 other visitors.

May 1 Tuesday	Letter from N.
May 2 Wednesday	Letter from N. F bought me violets.
May 3 Thursday	
May 4 Friday	L from N. Got up 11. 1st day up. Feeling pretty weak. Very hot weather. Lay on sofa with window wide open.
May 5 Saturday	Got up 11. Letter from N. F bought me primroses & sweets. F went to tennis. M & I started dressmaking.
May 6 Sunday	Lay on couch all day. Very lazy & stiff after standing 10 min yesterday.
May 7 Monday	Letter from N.
May 8 Tuesday	PC & letter from N.
May 9 Wednesday	Letter from N. Doctor O'Dowd came. Examined me. Much better.
May 10 Thursday	Letter from N. Came downstairs in the afternoon. M went to see *Daddy Longlegs*. M. Riddifan here for evening.

PART II:

AN OFFICER AND A GENTLEMAN

[Quite a few letters are missing from the start of Norman's time at Park Hall Camp, Oswestry, but Amiel's diary refers to receiving them on a regular and frequent basis still.]

Friday
[Oswestry, 4th May 1917]

My very own darling,

Very many thanks for your letter this morning, I am so glad you are better. Will you be quite well by tomorrow week do you think as I intended trying to get home for the weekend. Of course I may not be able to go but it is no use asking unless you are quite well again as I don't expect I shall be able to get much leave for a little while. I am going along here first rate and like the country round here immensely, it is almost as pretty as Hereford, but I do not think I am likely to meet any nice people here. I don't seem to have much time for going out, in fact I am more tied than I ever was before. But when you come here I must make a special effort.

You ask me to tell you everything about myself, well dearest – I do, there is very little to tell. All I do is feed, work and dream of you.

I can't get that song about Dixieland here. I am not sure of the title so I can't order it but we will get it when I come home. If it is a nice day tomorrow I hope to bike to Llangollen (9 miles) so if I don't get time for a letter please excuse me, but I will if I can. I do still love you even more than ever and I do wish I could have you on my knee and kiss you once again, don't you.

With all my love. Your own Norman.

Sunday
[Oswestry, 6th May 1917]

My own darling cherub,

Thank you very much for your letter yesterday; as it was such a lovely day I went out for the afternoon and did not return until it was too late for the post. It is a grand day again today and I am hoping to go out for a bike ride with another fellow here. He is a jolly nice chap and shares my room with me; he is married so he is not likely to lead me astray although that is not likely to happen. Just think, it is only a fortnight ago that I was with you and we went to the Botanical Gardens, it seems ages and ages since I kissed you, and I do miss it so very much. We must be brave and patient as I know that time makes no difference to us, but I shall be so glad when you have got that ring. When you write please don't be a bit afraid to put just what you think. Remember you are all mine and anything you say to me will be quite sacred and I shall be able to understand. It is so nice to hear you say how much you love me and want me, as you say I am sure we shouldn't get tired of each other and I am longing to hear you say you want to marry me. You will in all good time get like that, I know it is a great thing for a girl even more than for a fellow and love has to be very strong to feel like it, but you will feel that way in time.

I haven't forgotten Berkswell [pretty village near Hampton in Arden, Solihull] and what happened there, those were the happiest days . . .
[2ND PAGE MISSING]

10th May 1917
Park Hall Camp
Oswestry

My own love,

I was so pleased to get your letter today and to know you are going along so well and hope that by Saturday you will be quite yourself. I have got leave and hope to be at Snow Hill by 3.50 on Saturday and should like you to meet me there if you feel equal to it, after which you can come home to tea with me. If you are not there I shall quite understand and will come round to your house as soon after tea as possible. Should you be ill and unable to see me please wire me.

I am longing to hug you and have you on my knee again and I do hope you will be well enough for that because although I love you always and however you are, your kisses seem to bind us together tighter than ever. I shall have to go back first thing on Monday morning, but we shall have all Sunday together and it will be well worth it.

It is pouring with rain today, it has been rotten for us as we have had to stay indoors which I detest. How you have kept cheerful for 3 weeks I don't know. When I see you we can talk all about your coming here and try to convince your Father it is very necessary for both of us. I am afraid this is too late for tonight's post but I hope it reaches you in time.

I <u>do</u> hope I can come and that you will be almost well by then.
With all my love, Always your Norman.

Extract from Amiel's Diary

May 11 Friday	Letter from N. Practised. Wire from N. Coming today. Came 8.30. I feel very limp.
May 12 Saturday	Letter from N. Got up 9.30 N came. Lazy morning. Doctor came. Walk to Villa Cross with N & had music later.
May 13 Sunday	N came. This afternoon walked as far as Mrs Wells. Photos. Came home. F went cycle ride.
May 14 Monday	N caught 10.30 train to Oswestry. Warren, Brett & Povey came to tea. Jim & Rita to supper.

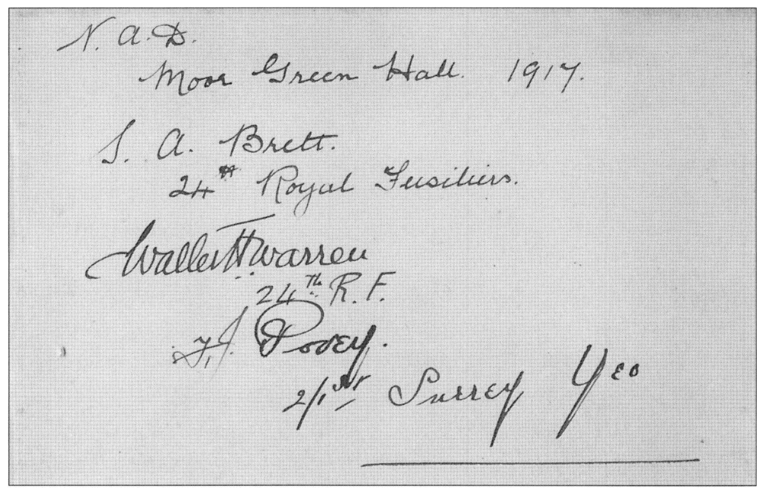

Autographs by Warren, Brett and Povey from Amiel's album.

Monday
[home, 14th May 1917]

My very own love,

I am just starting this before I leave home as it is so hard to write in the train. I don't want to leave you a little bit but I am heaps more cheerful than last time as I am hoping to have you with me again in a day or two.

I think it is awfully kind of your Father to let you both come, it will be very lonely for him, and you must mind you return looking very well so that he won't regret it.

You may be sure that tonight I shall do all I possibly can to get rooms for you so don't blame me if I can't because I do want to have you there, I want you more this time than I have ever done before and one reason is that I can see now you are quite settled.

Just keep cheerful even when I am not with you because it will soon all be over and I shall have you for ever then.

I am just going to the station now, and I hope to see you on Wednesday.
Give my love to your Mother and Father.

With all my love, Always your Norman.

Tuesday
[Oswestry, 15th May 1917]

My very own love,

I expect you will have received my wire and letter to your Mother by this time and hope you will come tomorrow. It is a fearful day today, raining hard, but we must hope that the weather will cheer up for you.

Tomorrow is always a bad day for me but I will spend as much time as I can with you. We have a lecture at 5.30 but I will try to run down to Whittington for a few minutes about 6.30, but I have to be in to dinner at 7 and cannot get excused as it is Mess Night, but other evenings I can get excused. I will come down after dinner of course.

I do want you here, I can hardly believe you are coming so soon, and if the weather is good I am sure you will have a good time and it will do you a lot of good.

I haven't much news as I shall be seeing you tomorrow, I hope, and I do love you darling, more than ever before.

With all my love, Always your own Norman.

[Amiel and her mother came to spend nearly a fortnight in Whittington, near Park Hall Camp, and Norman visited them when he was free of duties. He continued to write letters to Amiel during this time, and also wrote in her diary – writing as if he were she, but in pen instead of her pencil.]

Extract from Amiel's Diary

May 15 Tuesday	Letter from N. Wash day. Dressmakers. Fell down. M & F went to the Opera *Il Seraglio*.
May 16 Wednesday	Letter from N. M & I go to Whittington. Called at Mrs Wells first. N came about 6.30pm.
May 17 Thursday	[Ascension Day] Quiet walk with M. Lazy day. N came 6.30 Wet evening so stayed in.
May 18 Friday	M & I walked to Oswestry. Bought mat for N. Gathered primroses. At night N came.
May 19 Saturday	Letter from N. M & I sat sketching cottages. N & I went to Chirk Castle. Glorious afternoon. Came back 7.30. Supper 8.30
May 20 Sunday	Letters from Dot & Phillis Boyton. N & I cycled to Llangollen. Tea at Hand Hotel. Back 8. Quiet evening.
May 21 Monday	N called on his way to bombing at Fernhill. Picked ivy. N grubby

Amiel with the gathered primroses.

Mrs Robins and Amiel.

Norman and Amiel.

22nd May 1917
[Oswestry]

My own love,

Please forgive me for being so grubby last night, I really couldn't help it. There must have been something the matter with me as I couldn't get to sleep till about 2, a thing which never happens to me. Anyway I will try not to be so nasty again. It isn't that I love you any the less, I wanted you fearfully last night but couldn't somehow tell you, I don't know why.

I do hope I am forgiven.
With all my love, Always your Norman.

Friday
[25th May, Oswestry]

My own darling love,

I haven't got anything to write about but I know you like to have a letter from me. I can't look or think about next week as it will be awful without you; I quite feel you are part of me now and I can't let you go away. I <u>do</u> wish this war would finish so that I could have you for ever, but we must go on hoping.

With <u>all</u> my love. Always your own Norman.

Chaps throwing bombs.

Saturday
[26th May, Oswestry]

My very own love,

I thought I would just write a line to you to tell you once again how much I love you and I hope you will always want me as much as you do now. [He's just given Amiel an engagement ring earlier today.] The days seem awfully long without you and I am ever so glad when the time comes for me to come round to you. I only wish you could always be here. Always love me as you do now.

With all my love. Always your Norman.

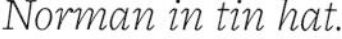

Norman in tin hat.

Cartoons of tin hat.

MAY	MEMS	1917	31 Days	CASH	MAY

20 SUN. Sunday after Ascension.
P.Cs from Dad & Phillis Boyton.
N & I cycled to Llangollen.
Tea at Hand Hotel. Back 8.
Quiet evening

21 MON. ● 0.47 a.m.
N called on his way to
Camping at Fernhill
Picked up. N grubby.

22 TUES.
Norman called. Letter.
Went to Canadian wedding,
Walked round N's camp.

23 WED. N called Photos tinted.
Painting all morning
" " " afternoon Saw
N for 2 min. He came 7.

24 THUR. Empire Day.
Went walk with N

25 FRI. Easter Law Sittings end.
Walked with N to
Oswestry

26 SAT. Queen born, 1867.
Went to Chirk with N he gave
me the long promised ring
which I wanted very much.
I am very happy & I know
he is & I shall be glad when I
get the other ring he will be.
I wish I could be here always
to look after him but I know
I can trust him

Page in Amiel's Diary showing Norman's writing.

MAY—JUNE MEMS 1917 | 31 & 30 Days CASH MAY—JUNE

27 SUN. Whitsun Day. Ember Week.
Rained hard, but had a lovely time with N, I am sure we shall be very happy.

28 MON. Whit Monday. Bank Holiday.
☽ 11.34 p.m.
Saw N in morning with his regiment. N went to Denbigh. I came home - 3.23
Must not be sad, because now I have got N.

29 TUES. Whit Tuesday. Stayed night at Wilsons. Back at Bank. [illegible] home from Grandfathers.
I know N is thinking about me today

30 WED. Ember Day. Letter from N.
Very busy straightening house. F & I went to see Mrs Wells. They are dears.
Liked my ring very much.

31 THUR. L from N
Wash day before Bank. Don't like bank or B'ham.

1 FRI. JUNE
Ember Day. L from N
Managed to get off to meet N's train & taxi up to Mrs Wells. Supper.
Talked. N brought me home. I didn't want him to go. Introduced him to [illegible]

2 SAT. Ember Day. L from N
N called at Bk. Photos printed & very nice too. N rang me up 2 o'clock. Balanced 2.15. Had
Coffee at Kardomah. Went to Mrs Wells for tea. We went to [illegible] pictures. N as usual behaved very badly. I came in 10.30

Page in Amiel's Diary showing Norman's writing.

Extract from Amiel's Diary

May 22 Tuesday	Norman called. Letter. Went to Canadian wedding. Walked round N's camp.
May 23 Wednesday	N called. Photo in tin hat. Painted all morning. Painted all afternoon. Saw N for 2 min. He came 7pm.
May 24 Thursday	[In Norman's writing] *Went walk with N.*
May 25 Friday	[In Norman's writing] *Walked with N to Oswestry.*
May 26 Saturday	[In Norman's writing] *Went to Chirk with N and he gave me the long promised ring which I wanted very much. I am very happy and I know he is and I shall be glad when I get the other ring and he will be. I wish I could be here always to look after him but I know I can trust him.*
May 27 Sunday	[In Norman's writing] *Rained hard but had a lovely time with N. I am sure we shall be very happy.*
May 28 Monday	[Bank Holiday] Saw N in morning with his regiment. M went to Denbigh. I came home 3.23pm. [In Norman's writing] *Must not be sad because now I have got N.*
May 29 Tuesday	Stayed night at Wilson's. Back at Bank. F home from Grandfather's. [In Norman's writing] *I know N is thinking about me today.*
May 30 Wednesday	Letter from N. Very busy straightening house. F and I went to see Mrs Wells. They are dears. Liked my ring very much.
May 31 Thursday	L from N. Washday before Bank. Don't like Bank or B'ham.

Amiel on a garden terrace.

Norman by a haystack.

Monday
[28th May 1917, Oswestry]

My very very own love,

I really don't know what to say to you now you have gone, I can hardly believe it is true and I have that nasty feeling in my tummy, but I must cheer up as I hope to be with you on Saturday.

We have had a lovely time haven't we and I hope it will be just the first of a life series of happy days for us. Now I have really got you I can tell you all my feelings and you know that I do love you, more every day I am sure.

I am sending this to the Bank so that you will get it earlier than at home. Be sure you write soon. I shall do so every day that I possibly can and I hope soon our writing days will be done for ever; when we have that

Today I am going out for a ride with Boyce, I feel so very lonely without you dearest and do hope I can have you for ever soon.

With all my love darling, Your very own Norman.

Norman weeping as Amiel leaves by train.

Tuesday
[29th May 1917, Oswestry]

My very own love,

Many thanks for your lovely letter this morning, it was a very happy surprise. I suppose you arrived home safely and I do hope you are cheerful. I can quite understand your feelings, I feel very much the same as you, except I still have that strange feeling in my tummy. I do so want you here darling; love is a fine thing but it does cause sadness. I have never missed you quite as much as I do now, but I must look forward to Saturday and you.

As I wanted to write to you yesterday we didn't go to Llangollen but only to Ellesmere. It was a fine ride and a big hill which I rode up (I don't think). There is a big lake there, just lovely it was and such a grand day, but all the while I was thinking of someone else although I tried to be cheerful. We must be thankful I am not abroad, I am near you if anything such as illness happens and I can come and see you occasionally. Your Mother was very good to me, I do hope she doesn't think I am ungrateful but I can't say the things I ought to in such cases.

I hope the Bank goes down alright, I would give a lot to have a kiss now but I must wait. You are all mine for always dearest and I shall do my utmost to make you happy and I shall always be true to you so don't worry.

With all my love, Always your very own Norman.
Just think – you are mine for all our lives darling xx

Tuesday evening [later that same day]

My <u>very own</u> love,

Although I have written to you once today, I so want to talk to you that I am starting tomorrow's letter tonight and I am sure you won't mind a bit. I am Orderly Officer for the next 3 days and I was so very afraid I should get it while you were here, as it was my turn some time ago, and it means that whoever does it has to stay in camp for the whole 3 days which would have upset our arrangements. It is so strange to be here and to keep thinking that you are gone. Often today I have quite forgotten that you have left me and keep wondering what you are doing at Whittington and then I realise that you are not there at all now. On this job there is very little to do, I don't go on parade at all but just look after various things in camp, so that I have really had too much time to think of things. We did have a lovely time didn't we? Now I look back on it I feel certain that it has been by far quite the happiest time in my life, and I hope in yours too. I shall never forget it, and particularly that great day at Chirk; I think we must always celebrate that day every year – May 26th – as it was then I felt for certain that I really loved you above everything else on earth and I also knew that you loved me. As I have told you, you are the one great ideal that I have and I am sure you will always be so.

I am very anxious to know what your Father thinks of the ring. It has occurred to me that I really ought to have written to him and asked his consent, but I felt that I already had it. I do hope he is not vexed about this, for as you know I do not want to displease him particularly as he has been so very kind and good to me.

I have asked for my leave but it is uncertain whether I shall get it yet but I am living in all hopes and will let you know as soon as I hear definitely. If I come, try to meet me and then you must come home with me – it will be the first time after becoming really mine. I hope you have gone to see Mother, she will be very glad to see you I know, for she thinks you are as good as I know you to be and that is saying a lot.

I won't write any more in this letter tonight but will continue in the morning. I do wish I could have just one kiss, I have got so that I can't do without them now. You know if you feel lonely and want me very much, you can always come to me whenever you please – we can soon fix up things and I am ready to have you just as soon as you like and I am sure your Father could soon be persuaded to agree when he sees how happy we are now.

Good night my own darling, the light has just switched off at the main so must stop. I sent you a goodnight kiss, love. x

Wednesday
I was rather disappointed at not having a letter this morning, but I expect it will come second post as you will have been busy. I have had lovely letters from Mother and Father about our engagement, they are both awfully pleased and want to see you very much, so I hope you will try to get round there as soon as you can.

I had a horrible dream about you last night, it didn't last long but I woke up feeling rotten and was so glad it wasn't real. It is too much to write here but I will tell you it when I see you which I hope will be this week. I am afraid I haven't much to say now and this is really quite a long letter.

With every bit of my love, Always your very own Norman.

Thursday
[31st May 1917, Oswestry]

My own dear love,

You will be very pleased to hear that if all goes well I hope to come home tomorrow – Friday – and you can expect me unless I have to wire you to the contrary. If you can, will you meet my train at Snow Hill [Birmingham city centre station] at 7.43 and then come straight home with me. I am ever so anxious to see you again and if you are not at the station I will come round to your house as soon as I have been home.

I was very glad to get your letter this morning and although it isn't nice to think you are sad yet I do feel happy to know you miss me and want me.

No darling, I never wish we hadn't met. I know just how you feel and I am just as lonely as you are, but it is worth bearing as we have got each other and someday, very soon I hope, we shall come to each other never to part again, and then I am sure we shall both be glad we have waited. That is, if we ever do think about it, as I know we shall be so very happy and have so much to do to keep us happy that we shall not want to think of days that are sad.

I am not going to write much tonight as I hope to be with you so soon now. I am so sorry to hear about the wrist watch, are you sure it is lost?

With all my love, Always your very own Norman.

How I feel tonight.

Norman arm in arm with Amiel wearing engagement ring.

Amiel and Norman in her parents' garden in Holly Road.

Extract from Amiel's Diary

Jun 1 Friday	L from N. Managed to get off to meet N's train and taxi up to Mrs Wells. Supper. Talked. N brought me home. I didn't want him to go. Introduced him to Mr W. [Possibly Mr Wayne, Dot's father?].
Jun 2 Saturday	L from N. N called at Bank. Photos painted and very nice too. N rang me up 2 o'clock. Balanced 2.15 Had coffee at Kahdomah [sic – there were two Kardomah Restaurants in the centre of Birmingham]. Went to Mrs Wells for tea. We went to Villa Cross pictures. N as usual behaved very badly. F came in 10.30pm
Jun 3 Sunday	F had dinner 9.30 Roast lamb, mint sauce, roast potatoes, maize pudding and rhubarb. N came 10. Spent day at Mrs Wells. Introduced to Miss Wells. [I can only guess that this might have been an aunt. Norman had no siblings.] Printed photos. N crumpled couch cover very badly, naughty little lad. Tea. Music. Supper. Came home 10.
Jun 4 Monday	Went to station & saw N off to Altcar 9am. In evening called at Griffins. M came back from Denbigh.
Jun 5 Tuesday	L from N. Show at Rugeley off. Went to Miss Reads. Dot stayed night. Jolly time.
Jun 6 Wednesday	L from N. Tickets for Theatre. Saw Mrs Wells for 3/4 hr. N's birthday.
Jun 7 Thursday	L from N. Allies at Churchfields. Motored there. Topping show. Went round the grounds before concert.
Jun 8 Friday	L from N. Busy at the office.
Jun 9 Saturday	L from N. M & I went to tennis 6 o'clock. Congratulations on all sides. Very nervous. Would love to have run away. Ethel Easy staying with Mrs Chirm.
Jun 10 Sunday	Letter fr N. Went to Griffins. Allies had about 60 photos taken in costume by Mr Yannold. Came home 9.40 M & F out.
Jun 11 Monday	L & PC from N. I took Bentley's place and balanced Postal Orders. M & I saw *The Rotters* at the Royal. Saw Marg Wildblood, Dot Lumley, Misses Dee. Congrats from all.
Jun 12 Tuesday	L from N. Allies show at Hampton. Very hot. Motored there. Great time.
Jun 13 Wednesday	L from N. M busy spring cleaning. Late at bank. Bed fairly early.
Jun 14 Thursday	PC from N. Miss Pilcher & I went to Mrs Sargeant in Acocks Green. Lovely time. Lovely house. Edith Strachan there. Tea in garden.
Jun 15 Friday	Letter from N. Busy day. Met Ethel Easy & M bought new blue costume at Stanley's. Called at Griffins 8pm. Gwen there also Harold. Mr & Mrs Griffins at Rhos [North Wales].

Amiel as 'England'.

Amiel as Burlington Bertie.

[Burlington Bertie from Bow *was written during the First World War by Williams Hargreaves for his wife Ella Shields, a vaudeville artist from America. It was a parody of an earlier song Burlington Bertie, and Ella always performed it in a slightly shabby dinner jacket and a dented topper. It became hugely popular. Vesta Tilley was another artist who impersonated men by wearing trousers and jackets – very risqué in the early 1900's, so Amiel is to be admired for being bold enough to dress and perform as a man and in front of soldiers!*]

'The Allies' as 'The Hotspurs' or 'Six Little Boys from School'.

'The Allies' in 'O Ebenezer O'.

Letter headed paper for School of Musketry.

Western Command School of Musketry
Altcar
Near Liverpool

Monday [4th June 1917]

My very own love,

You were a real darling to come to the station this morning, it did so cheer me up and also your lovely letter. I am writing this in the train and feel as though I don't want to leave my little cherub one bit. You needn't have any fears about being forgotten while I am down here, I am not quite like that as you ought to know by this time. I shall be so glad when all this war is done with and even if you are not ready to get married, we shall feel more settled and can look forward to it with more certainty than at present.

I do wish you were with me now, I am sure we should have a good time although of course it won't be quite a holiday as I expect I shall have quite a lot to do.

I have now just arrived. It is a topping place about 200 yds from the beach and my hut is very nice and comfortable and furnished and I am sure I shall be very happy. There are not many men here yet but they will roll up later I expect.

I find here a nice invite over to Southport this evening from my friends so I am sure I shall have a nice time. I <u>do</u> wish you were here dearest, it would be heaps nicer.

Be sure you write as often as you can and don't forget your little bunny.
With all my love, Always your own Norman.

Altcar
Tuesday [5th June 1917]

My own darling love,

I am afraid I have not such a lot to tell you today but I will do my best. After tea yesterday I went to Southport to see my friends; they are the parents of the girl who married Levason, who is killed. They were very pleased to see me and made me very welcome and I am to go there again.

We went for a long walk along the prom but there was no sea on view, it appeared to have all dried up. Lord Street is very fine and there is a topping band playing. I did wish you could have been with me, it seems rotten to have no-one to share all these pleasures with me, in fact I feel fearfully lonely particularly coming home. The fellow, Lloyd, who is sharing my room is out of the Herefords as I told you, and he is engaged and feels very much as I do. But it is nice having him with me as he can understand so well how I feel.

I was dreaming about you all last night, nothing very exciting but you were there all the while. Can't you feel ill again so that you would have to come down here, as apparently I shall get long evenings every day.

Levason's wife seems very well considering what she has gone through, but I don't think she realises that he is dead. She talks quite as though he were still in Egypt and that he is coming home soon. She seemed very bright and was pleased to see me again.

I do wish I could kiss you just once – I do love you angel as you know, so think of me. With all my love, Always your own Norman. xx

Altcar
Wednesday [6th June 1917, Norman's birthday]

My very own angel,

Thank you very very much for your good wishes and the lovely bookmark which I think is very clever, and also the most acceptable chocolate. It came at 11 this morning just when I was feeling hungry and I enjoyed some of it then and finished it this afternoon.

Oh darling I do so wish you were here, it is such a topping place, but it isn't a bit nice without you, I would much rather be in Handsworth just to have you. You have no idea how much I want you.

I have had several nice letters from people today and particularly Mother and Father who said some very nice things about both of us. Now that I have you, it has made this birthday heaps happier than any previous ones and I do hope by next one all this war is over and you will be my very own for ever.

I went into Southport again last night for a short time. There is an electric car runs from here and it only takes 15 minutes so I always feel it is worth going just to hear the band. There is an awfully good one in the winter gardens, all in red coats with gold braid and everything is lit up and looks so cheery after Oswestry and Birmingham. I haven't heard from my pal Price again but I am hoping to spend next Sunday with him at Wallasey. I haven't been to Liverpool yet, there doesn't seem much to do there unless it is to go to the theatre and I am sure I am not anxious to run into Enid, so don't worry about that dearest please.

Be sure you thank your Mother and Father for all their kind wishes. I am anxiously waiting for the ring, but don't hurry about it as it is sure to take some time.

I hope you had a nice time at Miss Read's. Have you been to tennis yet, I wonder if Kate is heartbroken that she has now lost me?

With all my love, Always your own Norman.

Altcar
Thursday [7th June 1917]

My very own darling,

Thank you very much for your nice long letter this morning and I am glad you still feel you want me with you, but that is only natural for both of us isn't it. I hope you went round to see Mother last night, I am sure she will be very glad to see you because as you know she is very fond of you. I had a very quiet day yesterday. It was guest night here so I stayed in to dinner and went into Hightown. This is the nearest town to the camp, it is only very tiny with about two shops, but there are some topping little houses, just the sort we shall want and it made me think a lot about you and the times we shall have when all this business is finished. The revolver course which I am doing now is very interesting but I am afraid I am not much of a shot, I am much more at home with a rifle, but I am sure I shall learn a lot here, they are very thorough. We don't have very long hours, only 9 to 12.30 and 2 to 4, so if you were here we could have even a longer time together than at Whittington. I am sure I shall never forget those very happy days; whenever I smell lilac I think of that bush in front of the house. Tonight my friends have invited me to Southport again and I shall go but it is not very exciting as they are old, but still there is usually a good feed.

I shall get quite lazy if I stay here long as I never think of getting up before 7.30 and I sleep like blazes, it must be the sea air. The weather has not been very settled, it was pouring early this morning but looks as though it will cheer up tonight. I do so miss you and I do love you darling.

With all my love. Always your own Norman.
Don't forget to get my

1. Tennis racket.
2. Films, before my folks go away.

Altcar
Friday [8th June 1917]

My own darling love,

I don't really know how to thank you for that lovely ring. I do like it immensely and it fits perfectly. I don't think it is a bit too big and I am sure I shall never take it off now I have put it on, only I wish you could have put it on for me. I quite expected it this morning as last night I dreamed you sent me one but I didn't like it a bit. It was an awfully strange one and we finally decided to change it but you seemed rather to like it. And when I went into breakfast there was this lovely one all waiting for me.

I went over to my friends house last night and they had some very jolly people there. We all went to the Palladium Music Hall after a good feed and I enjoyed it immensely. I expect you will think I am having a very lively time, I certainly am but you needn't be a bit afraid that I am forgetting my angel, because you are <u>always</u> in my thoughts. All the time last night I was wishing you could have been with me and then it would have been really extra.

The weather is not over good again today and I am afraid I am not getting very brown but it generally clears off for the evenings and that is the main thing. On

Sunday I am spending the day with my old pal Price and I shouldn't wonder if you aren't mentioned perhaps just once or twice – it is quite probable.

I do hope you can help Dot along a bit, I am so sorry about that; but if we were ever similarly placed I should try to persuade you to get married at once although let us hope nothing does happen that way to us.

With ever so much love and kisses for the ring which I am sure will help to keep us even closer now.

Always your very own Norman.

Altcar
Saturday [9th June 1917]

My very own love,

I didn't have a letter from you this morning but I expect perhaps you were late at the office and didn't get a chance to write. I am writing this on the shore at Altcar as we are waiting to fire and it is absolutely lovely here, I do wish you were here. It is hot and very sunny and the sand is warm but it would be heaps and heaps nicer with you here although I expect you would feel a bit bashful as there are about a dozen officers with me, but still we could easily lose them among these sand hills.

Last night I went over to see Mrs Levason's people again but somehow I didn't enjoy it much, I think it is seeing them all in black it got on my nerves and I did feel as though I wanted you as well. Southport looked extra, it was a topping evening and the sea was very blue. We have just rescued a young lark from a lizard. The mother is anxiously looking for it but I think she has just found it, we put it out in the sun.

Today I am going to see Price and I feel quite excited about it, and I am sure he is.

My ring looks lovely and makes me think of you even more than before but it does make me want you here.

I am afraid I haven't time to write anymore today, there isn't very much to say but I hope you will have a good weekend I know I shall but it won't be as nice as last, that seems ages ago and I do hope it won't be long until I see you again.

I <u>do</u> love you.
With all my love, Always your own, Norman.

Altcar
Sunday [10th June 1917]

My own love,

I am so sorry to hear you were feeling fed up on Friday night; it is strange but I felt just the same. It seems funny that we can't have feelings without the other one getting them but I suppose it will be alright when we are married. Now darling when you do feel lonely and depressed, you must try to cheer up because I know just what it feels like and it is rotten. Sometimes I feel I do so want you with me – more than you can tell, and it is then I have to cheer myself up with the thought that some day I shall have you for ever and ever. So always remember you have got me and all my love and let us try to be happy in looking into the future and thinking about our new home.

I went over to see Price yesterday and we had a fine time together. I am spending the day there again today.

He is in hospital about 5 minutes from his home but seems to get out as much as he likes. He hasn't lost his right arm although it was a very near thing, and he doesn't think it will ever be any use again. He has had some fearful experiences, but we talked chiefly about you and someone he knows, and Hereford. He thinks I am very lucky to have got you and so do I but I wish the war were over all the same and then I could have you for ever.

With all my love. Always your very own Norman.
I think the flowers are called Birdseye. They are very common here but pretty I think. xxx

Altcar
Monday [11th June 1917]

My own darling love,

I was disappointed at not getting a letter this morning but am expecting one tonight as probably the posts are upset again.

I had quite a nice day again with Price yesterday at his place. I went to his hospital in the morning and then to his place to dinner where we had a <u>good</u> <u>feed</u>. After a rest we walked out to some place along the shore and had tea. I did wish you could have been there, it was absolutely lovely and hot and the sea looked extra. He seems to be having a very good time but he deserves it as he has been through a fearful lot before he came home, and his right hand will never be of much use again.

I was dreaming of you again last night but cannot remember details. The great disadvantage of loving you is that I want you always here and it makes me feel lonely sometimes, but I just look at my ring and that seems to be a bit of you so I cheer up then. It looks topping now, the new gilt is wearing off and the gold is showing up properly. I do like it.

I must go now darling but you know I do so love you even more than when I was with you last.
With all my love. Always your own, Norman.

Altcar
Wednesday [13th June 1917]

My own darling love,

I was so glad to get a letter this morning, do you know I haven't had one since Sunday and that was posted on Friday, I began to feel sure you must be bad. I am still having quite a decent time here, I had a day's holiday yesterday as I had finished my first course, and I went to Liverpool in the morning and had a fine time sailing backwards and forwards over the river. I quite imagined I had joined the navy.

In the afternoon I went to my friends at Southport and we all went to a fine place in the country to tea. The country round here is not very attractive and I prefer Oswestry to it for scenery, but of course I do like the sea and shall miss it fearfully when I leave here. I wish I could get a job here for the duration.

There is no bathing at Altcar as the sands are very dangerous and I have been too lazy to do any at Southport although I must go in before I go from here.

You seem to be having a very good time in the office, how is it Dot manages to pinch a day off when she likes, I think you had better do that and come down to Whittington for a weekend shortly. Saturday afternoon to Monday would be well worth it and very nice too, and I am sure your Father wouldn't mind your being alone for that short time now we are as we are.

Be sure you write to me often as I do so look forward to your letters and it is such a disappointment when there isn't one.

With all my love, Always your own, Norman.

Altcar
Thursday [14th June 1917]

My very own love,

I am having a quiet evening tonight and thought I would stay in and go to bed early as it has been so terribly hot today I feel quite tired.

I went into Liverpool yesterday to meet Price and ran across Enid. I was very surprised to see her as it is such a big place I never thought I should and as you know I said I should not write and ask her to meet me again.

She liked my ring very much and also the photo of you. I am sure she is not a bit keen now and I am very glad as I should hate to feel she was miserable on my account. I was only with her a short while as she had an appointment and I am not likely to see her again.

Meeting her did not affect me in the least, as I told you before I am quite certain of myself and I know you are.

I am afraid I shall not see you for some time as Mother and Father think of remaining in Llandudno until about July 5th so although I could get a weekend they won't be at home to look after me. Never mind, time soon flies and I shall have you with me soon again.

I am just waiting for dinner now and I do wish I were going to Whittington afterwards to see you. I never can forget those days and if our honeymoon is as happy I shall be quite contented but I expect it will be even happier although we can't imagine it.

I don't seem to get very brown here although it has been very hot and sunny but I still live in hopes.

Have you got those photos yet, be sure you let me know and did you get my racquet? You are a silly cherub if you didn't as it would be useful to you.

Give my love to your Mother and Father and heaps and heaps for you darling.
Always your very own Norman.

I do so love you angel. Goodnight love xx

Altcar
[Friday] 15th June 1917

My own darling Cherub,

Your letter arrived safely yesterday and I was very glad to get such a nice long one. There wasn't one this morning but I think you had a show on.

Those letters you sent never reached me and there were one or two more from other people that haven't turned up, I don't know how it has happened. I expect I shall get them about 1961 if they have gone astray.

Your Mother has written and asked me to come and stay with you on the 23rd weekend, so if you haven't got anything fixed up I know you would like to have me. You have a show on I know but perhaps you will let me come and see it. You mustn't be shy that time or you will get smacked.

You ask me to tell you all about my work here, well I am afraid it wouldn't be very interesting. We have heaps of lectures and tons of notes but it is such a very technical subject I shall have to wait until I see you to explain it. It is all about angles and triangles and other bogie things and we use heaps of very long words, so altogether I am beginning to feel very brainy.

Last night I went to the pictures and enjoyed them very much. The last time I went was with you and I did think about it. My old friend Chas. Chaplin was on and some of the films were extra, but the place was not so good as at Villa Cross or the Scala [probably the former cinema in Smallbrook Street, Birmingham city centre, opened in 1914.]

Tomorrow I hope to see Price again if fine.
With all my love. Always your very own Norman.

Me working tonight.

Extract from Amiel's Diary

Jun 16 Saturday	
Jun 17 Sunday	L from N. Ethel here. M & she went to band. Jim B & Rita to tea. E & I went to Mrs Chirm's later. Stayed supper.
Jun 18 Monday	L from N. Quiet day.
Jun 19 Tuesday	L from N. Singing lesson in town. Theatre *The Rotters*. M & F went also.
Jun 20 Wednesday	L from N.
Jun 21 Thursday	L from N.

Altcar
Saturday [16th June 1917]

My very own love,

Thank you very much for your letter this morning, there was no reason for you to tick me off about asking about the photos because I never received your letter saying you had them or enclosing a letter to Mother.

I am sure she would like to hear from you and her address is:
Westward Ho, Augusta Street, Llandudno
I cannot understand why those letters never came here, you have no idea how worried I was when I never heard for about 5 days, but they are alright again now.

Last night I stayed in and worked until late then I went for a fine long walk, but all alone. I did wish you were there as we should have been happy together shouldn't we? I walked about 8 miles and found a topping little inn for supper where I had some 'am, and gooseberry pie, which was extra.

I am glad you had such a nice time with Mrs. Sargeant, don't you worry we shall be heaps happier than they are. Now don't forget to write and let me know about next weekend. As I told you I had no intention of meeting Enid here and I only did so quite by accident so don't be grubby please, I was only with her about 2 minutes but don't suggest that you don't mind my seeing her because you do, at least you ought to. I do love you and only you darling.

With all my love. Always your own Norman. xxxx
Thank you for the bit of poetry it was very nice.

Altcar
[Sunday] 17th June 1917

My own darling love,

You will be glad to know that this morning I received **3** long letters from you dated the 11th, 12th and 16th so you can see that on the 11th and 12th I didn't get any. The one is a lovely long one, I do wish I could write such nice letters as you do, they always make me feel so very sure of your love. I will send on the enclosure to Mother.

Ain't it 'orrid 'ot. Yesterday I was absolutely baked and fell nearly asleep all the morning; it was much nicer at New Brighton in the afternoon as I managed to keep fairly cool. I did wish you could have been there, I like the place ever so much and it was absolutely crowded. There are heaps of wounded about, there must be a lot of hospitals there.

I do hope I can get over next weekend. I shall not be able to come until Saturday but considering that I shall not have to leave you at all we shall have quite as much time together as we usually get. If it is all the same to you I would much rather have your little bedroom. For one reason it is yours and I would always rather sleep alone. But I will do just what will suit your Mother best and I can always sleep anywhere.

You mustn't think too much about my coming as of course I don't know for certain, but I live in hopes and I am just dying to kiss you again.
You talk about getting up early, you wait until I come and if you are not out very early just look out.

Just try and be cheerful darling while I am away from you. I know how hard it is for me when I want you so much, but we can't help it. When I come over we will have another talk about things and if you are ready darling you know I am, but I want you to be quite happy about it, so think it out. I have met several nice people here and they all think we should be so much happier if you and I were together always and of course we should.

Don't think I want to persuade you against your will because I don't; I only say I am ready just when you are.

I have got to work hard this morning – Sunday – bad lad – but I have been out so much that I am afraid I have neglected the work a bit.

I am leaving here Wednesday afternoon and then I shall soon see my little Cherub I hope. With all my love. Always your own Norman.

Next Saturday.

Altcar
Monday [18th June 1917]

My very own darling,

Please excuse the very grubby bit of notepaper but it is the only sheet I can find at present. I haven't had a letter this morning but as three came yesterday I must be content. What a beautiful long one there was too, I did so enjoy reading it, only it always makes me want to have you here.

The tennis folks are very good to take such an interest in us, and why Horace Wall should feel like giving me a good character I don't know. I am sorry I did not tell you about the soda for the photos, but you see it wasn't my fault, the letters hadn't arrived.

I had a very nice day yesterday. I worked until about 11.30 and then it looked so beautiful outside I felt I really couldn't stay in any longer so I went out with my pal here to Southport. We had dinner at a fine hotel and had a grand feed after which I wanted to sleep but didn't. It was terribly hot in the afternoon so we went to my friends' house and lay in the garden in the shade, and we stayed to supper.

I am sorry my course is coming to an end, I leave here Wednesday, but I shall soon see you again I hope. I know Formby very well, it is the next station to Altcar and I often walk over there.

Tonight I am going to have my hair cut ready for seeing you on Saturday, as at present it is all on my shoulders – there is much too much for you to pull as it is now. xxxx
With all my love. Always your very own Norman.

Before and after my haircut.

Altcar
[Tuesday] 19th June 1917

My very own love,

I quite expected a nice long letter this morning and was very disappointed when nothing came. You haven't written since Saturday, at least no letters have reached me and I do so miss them.

There isn't very much to write about except that yesterday and today I have felt that I wanted you here more than usual. Sometimes I feel I would give anything to have you and I shall be so glad when the war is over so that we can fix things up. I am looking forward to Saturday, it won't be long now and when I get back tomorrow I shall put in for leave and will let you know the time the train comes in.

I shall be sorry to be back at Oswestry for some things, but I shall feel I am nearer to you and I shall have the old spots to visit once more.

I went to the pictures last night but didn't care for them much as they were very exciting and I have had a headache for the last few days. I think it must be the hot sun and no exercise.

I expect Price will come down to Birmingham to stay with me when he is better so you will see him then.

Has Mrs Easy been staying with you, and why should she not like your being engaged? If her life hasn't been over happy don't dearest think we need be like it, it will be our own fault if we are and I do love you and you do me I know. You are so very different from any other sort of girl and that is why I love you so much.

It will soon be Saturday and then I can really love you once more as much as we like. I am just longing for a kiss from my angel.
With all my love. Always your own Norman.

Altcar
[Wed] 20th June 1917

My own dear love,

I was so glad to have a letter this morning, I hadn't had one since Sunday and I began to wonder if anything was the matter.

As regards the weekend I am afraid it is impossible for me to come before Saturday, in fact as yet I can't say for certain whether I shall get leave but we must live in hopes. Anyway you may be sure I shall do all I possibly can to come and as early as possible as I do so want to be with you again. It is all very well being here, I have certainly had a good time but it hasn't been a quarter as nice as that fortnight at Whittington.

I am sorry if I haven't answered your questions. You see I often have to answer your letters when I haven't them with me and that is how it happens I expect, but you must write out a long list of things to ask me when I come over and we can see into them then.

I am sure we shall have a nice time at the Bot. Gardens. [Botanical Gardens, Birmingham.] I am very anxious to see the show and it will be extra not having to leave you at night as we usually do.

Don't forget that Oswestry will be my address now.

With every bit of love. Always your very own Norman.
I think I want you more now than I have ever done xxxxxxx

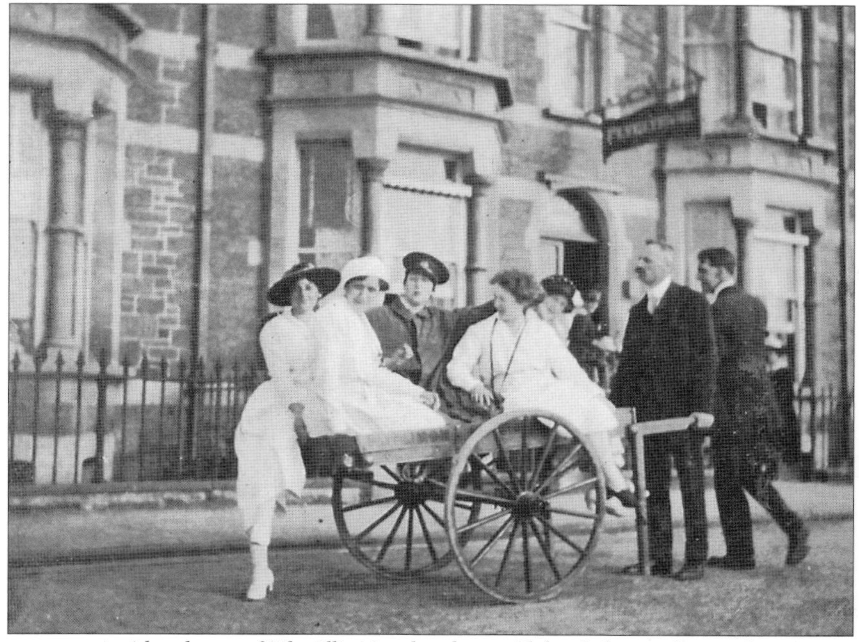

Amiel and some of 'The Allies' in a handcart with her father ready to push.

The National Anthems of the Allies.

BRITAIN

GOD SAVE THE KING

FRANCE

THE MARSEILLAISE

BELGIUM

THE BRABANÇONNE

RUSSIA

GOD SAVE THE TSAR!

JAPAN

National Anthem, KIMI-GA-YO

COPYRIGHT.

National Anthems of The Allies.

Amiel in 'Me an' Mrs 'ide'.

Extract from Amiel's Diary

Jun 22 Friday	(Longest Day.) So it was. Came home for tea. Bought hat. Met N's train 7.40. Supper. N & I went to Griffins. Saw Allies photos. Lovely to have N again. 12 Bed.
Jun 23 Saturday	N came into office. I left 10 o'clock. Dinner. Rest. Botanical Gardens 4.30pm. Tea show 5.30pm & 7.30pm N sent me up some tea. It was good. Box of chocs. Came home 10.15pm. Supper. Quiet time. Bed.
Jun 24 Sunday	Got up 10. M & F breakfast in bed. 1st breakfast with N. Walked to his house. Mr & Mrs Wells still at Llandudno. Quiet afternoon in billiard room. Mr Clarke came. Walk. Mrs Coates and C came. Bed 12.
Jun 25 Monday	N came to town 9.10. I met him 10 o'clock. Train to Oswestry 10.40 Walked round, he brought me red roses. Dear old thing. I do hate him to go back.
Jun 26 Tuesday	(Mrs Chirm's birthday) Letter from N. M & F came to town. Tickets for *Her Husband's Wife*. Dot and I got in for 2nd act. Very good. M had letter from N as well.
Jun 27 Wednesday	L from N. Busy till 10pm.
Jun 28 Thursday	L from N. Balance. Went home with Mrs Featherstone Haugh 10.30pm.
Jun 29 Friday	L from N. Mr Peverall and F came into Bank. No work. I stayed till 8. Went to Wilson's. Mrs Wilson from Bradford, Uncle Len & Aunty Maggie. Motored home. Mr P stayed the night.
Jun 30 Saturday	[no more entries until 11th July.]

Park Hall Camp
Oswestry
[Monday] 25th June 1917

My very own love,

I have only two minutes before the post goes but I knew you would be glad to know that I got back here safely. The train came in exactly as you left me and I had quite a good journey down, meeting Boyce at Shrewsbury.

I am so glad I came, I have always wanted to see you in your home, it is always so different from just going in for a few minutes, and it has made me love you much more than I did before.

I am <u>so</u> sorry to know you think I am selfish. I always told you I was but I really mean to improve if I can, I do want you to help me with it. You know you can influence me by your love and we shall be much happier if you do. Don't get a serious little cherub; if I could be with you I would see you didn't, and don't worry about me, you have really got me and I have you for ever now so smile duckie. I will write more tomorrow.

With all my love, Always your own, Norman
Photo by Price enclosed. [Unknown photo.]

Oswestry
Tuesday [26th June 1917]

My very own love,

I expect you went to the theatre last night as there was no letter this morning, did I tell you that one dated the 17th arrived yesterday. Last night we were supposed to go to the trenches for night work but for once our luck was in and it rained cats and puppy dogs just when we should have started so we didn't go. I was very glad although I expect we shall have to go tonight but I was feeling tired and went to bed at 9.30.

We have a new idea since I have been at Altcar and that is that the men don't come back to dinner but have some bread and jam or cheese out wherever they are. It sounds very nice but I do get most awfully hungry on bread and cheese and I expect the men do. Today we started on the same game but at 11 we had a fearful storm and had to return so here I am. When we get to Swansea I expect I shall be going out fairly soon but somehow now I don't mind a bit; after seeing you last weekend I feel so very settled and seem to know that your love will last for ever. If I had gone without being certain of this it would have made the trials seem much harder but it is all so different now.

Today I have felt rather fed up, I expect it is work again, but I am quite happy knowing I have your love and I hope very soon to be with you again.

There isn't very much to write about, the rain kept us in last night but I am quite happy in camp thinking about you. Be sure you don't overdo it at the Balance, and try to write regularly as I so long for letters from you. Ask as many questions as you like and I will really try to answer them. I am trying to be a more considerate lad now so try me.

With all my love, Always your own, Norman.

Oswestry
Wednesday
[27th June 1917]

My own dearest Angel,

I was so glad to have that lovely letter from you today, if you knew how much they cheered me up you would send umpteen daily but I will excuse you so long as I get just one. Of course during the Balance I know it will be a job to find time to write but a postcard will do so long as I get something from you.

You are a funny cherub to change into my bed, but I know it made all the difference to me when I thought that you had been in it. It was so much nicer to have you in the house with me and if it can be managed, the next time I come home you must stay at my place.

You have no reason to be sorry for your behaviour on Sunday, surely it is only right and natural for you to be upset when I have to leave you; you would surely not be very much in love if you didn't. I know if I could give way like you did, it would ease my feeling very often, I get that rotten feeling in the tummy and all seems black without you. Never mind darling, I am sure we shall find it has all been worth waiting for, nothing is worth having unless we have to suffer to get it, and that is how I feel about our little home just for us two. Be sure you always tell me just how you feel, if you can't tell me everything, who else is there as we seem to be very close to one another now don't you think?

It has rained again very hard today and looks as though it won't leave off again. Last night Boyce and I walked round Whittington; it was a grand evening and we saw a fine sunset, it quite got us down, and all the flowers smelt extra. I should have liked to have got a huge lot of roses and sent them to you, but it is so difficult to keep them until I get a chance of going into town to the Post Office.

I will let you have another letter tomorrow. Take care of yourself darling during the hard Balance cos I do love you and I do want you.

With all my love. Always your own Norman.

Oswestry
Thursday [28 June 1917]

My very own love,

I hope you don't mind this being written in pencil but the ink is nearly dry and I can write so much more like this. Thank you very much for sending the collar and that lovely long letter, it did so cheer me up although since I last saw you I have felt very settled and happy. I was glad to know you got to the theatre, you don't say whether it was good but the title doesn't sound over attractive. Everyone seems trying to make you happy at the Bank, but who could help it when they know what a darling you are.

You are a silly old coon to worry over saying what you did to me. We can't always feel as though everything is right, I am sure I don't but we must live in the knowledge that we have got each other and as soon as we really can realise that, I am sure we shall be happy. We are really being tested very much and shall be more so when I leave England but always try and think as I do that <u>whatever</u> happens we belong to each other. You know what it says on the marriage service, something about 'in health or sickness, riches or poverty, for better or worse' and that is how I feel about you because I know it is true and you know you have me that way too. Always try to remember that my darling and it will often cheer you up when perhaps things seem a bit rotten and you feel you must have me with you to be happy.

I often get fed up with things here, chiefly the uncertainty of everything and it always helps me to see things clearer if I turn up some of your old letters. That letter that came about 10 days late I haven't opened yet but I know it is sure to be full of love so I am keeping it for a particularly dark day and I shall then have something quite fresh to put me right again.

Last night it poured in torrents so we decided to get up a concert to cheer up the men. It was quite a scratch affair but the men enjoyed it very much I think. I did the accompanying and sang one or two things from memory as I had no music here. Now if you could have just sung one or two, particularly in the 'more or less' costume, what a concert we could have had. Why you didn't want me to see you in those togs I can't think, you surely don't think I am narrow minded in such matters and would be shocked. I love you and understand you too well to know that you would never do anything that wasn't quite as it should be, so why did you think I might object?

I am so glad you cheered up poor Dot, she is having a rotten time but it will all come right. Always make her believe that she must stick to Aubrey for ever, she can't possibly give him up now. If they love in any way like us it would break both their hearts.

Goodnight my darling, xxxxxx Always your very own Norman.

Park Hall Camp
Oswestry
[Friday] 29th June 1917

My own darling cherub,

I expect you have started working late in real earnest as there was no letter for poor little me this morning. It does seem lonely when one doesn't come, but I can quite understand how it is so just do the best you can.

I went to the camp theatre last night to see a concert party called *Vogue*. They were really topping, one of the very best shows of its kind I have ever seen, and I did wish you could have been there to enjoy it with me.

They had some awfully good new numbers but as most of them were original we shall not be able to get them. One girl sang *So He Followed Me* out of *The Bing Girls* and it would do awfully well for *The Allies*. It is quite saucy and a lot of work for the troupe in it.

Mother is going home next Wednesday and she wants you to call as soon as you can get round, so be sure you go and you can help to cheer up one another.

I quite thought we should be moving to Swansea this weekend but now it does not look as though we shall go until next week. I shall be jolly glad when it is all over as a move means such an extra lot of work and it seems to go on to all hours of the night. I don't suppose I shall be lucky enough to stay in England much longer as all the fit officers will be moved when we leave here. For most things I shall be glad to go out as I don't feel it is a bit right for me to be here while heaps of my pals are having to go through it, but I do hope you won't worry about me as it will be so much harder for me. I know how you must feel because I know how I should be if you had to be out there, but I am usually fairly lucky and it will soon be all over now. Remember wherever I am I shall love you just the same as I do now. I feel sure my love won't alter a bit unless it grows keener, which it seems to do at present. I am Orderly Officer for the next three days so there will be nothing much to write about as regards work, I have to just stay about the camp in case an officer is wanted for an emergency.

I have met an awfully nice fellow here, he is just back wounded from France. We seemed to pal up at once, his name is Knapp.

Please write when you can and remember angel I do love you.
With all my love, Always your own, Norman.

Park Hall Camp
Oswestry
Sat. evening [30 June 1917]

My very dearest girl,

You can't tell how glad I was to get such a lovely letter from you this evening and I never expected it as your card came this morning. I am so glad you feel cheerful and are not worrying, and I do hope you will keep like it even when I leave England, which of course can't be so very far off now. It does so help me to get along if I know you are patient and just loving me wherever I am. I can't think how you came to write a beastly letter but I wish you had sent it all the same, with the one you did send of course.

I can't really imagine you writing a rotten letter and I am sure it wasn't so very terrible really. Of course neither of us can always feel just the same about anything and it is useless to think that we are each marrying angels, although I really do think darling you are very near to being one – to me you are.

Why should you be so afraid to own your love to me; surely we know each other by this time and I am sure you can't lose any womanliness by telling your future husband that you love him. So you really think dearest I would have got engaged to you if I hadn't felt quite certain that you wanted me, it would have worried me fearfully if I didn't know for sure. But thank goodness I do know that your love for me is true and lasting and I hope you know the same about mine. All the same we must be prepared for conflicting thoughts and also other people trying to point out that love like ours is foolish; but we know in our hearts what will make us happiest so why trouble about other folks' opinions. Take it from me darling, no-one understands love except the two people it concerns, even our parents don't see it quite as we do, so never worry about any ideas of other people or of the other Amiel which is really only a conventional mood you catch from being with other folks. I love you as much as I am capable of doing and although I know it is not great or good enough for you, yet I do hope it will increase as I try to get more unselfish. I am sure that when we live together we get like one another in character, so then I shall get more like my angel and shall be more capable of loving her. Don't think I don't love you dearly because you know I do, but you are always telling me I don't love you sufficient. I always imagine I couldn't love anyone more than I do you, but I expect you are right and it will grow in time. Hardships work wonders and I expect I shall have my share in good time. Now I know you are mine I am honestly keen to go out. I am sure it will do me good and make me more worthy of you and I don't feel I shall have done my duty until I have gone. But still it isn't in my power to go or stay away of course.

I am glad the Balance seems going so well and that you got away fairly early. I have not gone out as I am Orderly Officer but tomorrow I am going out to supper with the fellow Knapp I told you about. He knows some people here who have asked us round. I know where they live, I think the other side of the town. He is an awfully decent chap and thinks you must be extra – are you?

You see I have written in pencil again, and I hope it has not been too long for you, but I expect not, if you like letters as much as I do. It is late now so I won't post this until Sunday morning in case I don't get time to write then. I should just like to have three minutes alone with you in the drawing room – but the time will come and soon I hope.

Goodnight my own love and may our love keep as sincere as it is today, but I am sure it will. Do you know we have got at least 60 years to be together never to leave each other for a day – it doesn't seem possible. Never mind, very nice too.

With all my love, Always your own Norman.

Oswestry
Monday [2 July 1917]

My very own love,

I am ever so disappointed that there was no letter from you today or yesterday, if you knew how I looked for them I am sure you would write a wee postcard or something, but I live in hopes to have one tomorrow.

I had a very jolly time last night at that house where I said I was going. There we met several people there including a fellow I know in the Monmouths and his wife. She was the image of you only very fair, and I felt all funny when I saw her come in she was so like you. She was of course awfully nice and I did envy him being married. They live in rooms at Whittington and he goes home to sleep every evening. I sang one or two songs and played some accompaniments and did wish you could have been there. I am going again on Thursday to play tennis if we have not moved. I might also add we had a grand feed.

Now darling do hurry up and write or I shall begin to think that Dot has influenced your love in some way – but I don't think that is very likely now – if it is it mustn't occur or you know you will be smacked. Don't overwork yourself.

With all my love, Always your very own Norman.

Oswestry
Tuesday [3 July 1917]

My own darling angel,

You can't tell how glad I was to get your nice long letter this morning, you seem to be having quite a decent time in spite of the Balance and I am sure it was a good thing I wasn't at your house this weekend if you didn't get up until 3.45, but I should have turned you out long before then – really!

I apologise for not thinking that was Harold Hollins, you certainly are right – sometimes, and that was one of the times, but he has altered a lot since I last saw him – I will allow you to ruffle my hair once as punishment, and I sit at present in a feeling of sackcloth and ashes.

Re your £3 3/- present, such a large sum is outside the limits of my ideas of presents, 2/6 is about my limit so please appeal to a mightier brain. But seriously darling it was awfully good of Mr Oldfriend, and how about those old plate candlesticks or something like that if you feel so disposed.

You certainly mustn't fall in love with Mr F.W. I should hate to hurt him but if you make such suggestions it will have to be done – let us hope he doesn't come to an untimely end through the fickleness of woman. He certainly is a decent boy I should think but you are mine now and for ever so just show him this picture of me drawn from life. [F.W. may have been the F. Wright referred to in Amiel's diary dated 20th September]

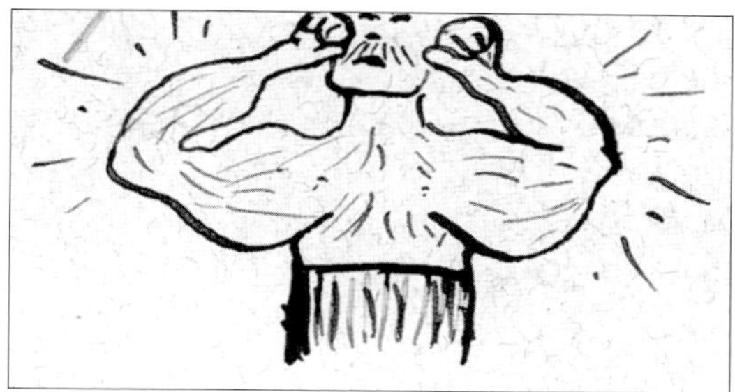

Cartoon of Norman flexing his biceps.

Photo of Norman in the centre of his men.

We have had a very exciting day today, Sir [William] Pitcairn Campbell, a full blown general, [General Officer Commander in Chief, Western Command 1916-18] and all the brass hats of the War Office have been down to inspect us, and the 'wind up' has been most intense. It all went off satisfactorily and I had a long talk with him, that is comparatively speaking – about 20 words, so my future is now assured. I feel jolly tired and it was awfully hot but everyone went away pleased.

I do hope you will not look upon marriage as giving up your freedom. You are a strange little cherub but all the same you are everything in the world to me. We are sure to be happy together and it should mean that we are both more free to enjoy ourselves and do as we like. Surely we are always happiest when we are together and so why shouldn't we enjoy life more after marriage than before. All our joys will be doubled and our troubles halved. All the same I am contented to wait until you feel ready, but when you are I am and I hope it won't be so very very long.

Don't be surprised if a little parcel comes for you tomorrow, let me know if it doesn't; don't expect another diamond ring but it is only . . . my word, isn't she curious.

Shall you be in this weekend as I might, a very bit might, come and see you, but don't build on it as all is very uncertain owing to the move. In any case I couldn't arrive until 3.45 Saturday, so push on with the DCAs and what's on at the theatres. Don't expect me, but live in hopes.

It is Mother's birthday on Wednesday so call as soon as you can.

I do so love you angel. Don't think I want to rush you into marriage, your happiness must come before all – but when you are ready I am.

With all my love, Always your own Norman.

Sir William Pitcairn Campbell.

Oswestry
Wednesday night [4 July 1917]

My very own love,

You will be as disappointed to hear as I am that we are moving on Saturday next to Swansea and after that day my address will be:

1st Herefords, Sketty Park, Swansea

and this will mean that our hopes of the weekend are now poo. I am very upset about it as I did so want to see you but you may be sure I shall come as soon as I possibly can.

I don't want to worry you and please don't say much about it at home but I think you ought to know that now I feel that my time in this country is fairly short. I honestly want to get out particularly as I feel so sure of your love. You wouldn't like it all to end and think that your husband had not done his share – just think it over, and I feel I ought to go although of course it is nothing to do with me in the least, so write and say you agree with me. It will test our love I know, if we are separated for long but I am quite sure of myself and of you so however long we are apart we shall come together just the same. I shall of course see you heaps of times before then as I shall worry for leave as soon as we get settled and I do hope to come Saturday week if I can.

Thursday [continuation of above letter]
I got your cheery letter this morning and it did me a lot of good. Although you write and say I am not selfish I know very well that I am and if you really can't see it, it is only because you love me so much. I do wish I could be in the office to help you, if things are really as bad as you say, but old Mr Price always tries to make out he is overdone and I am afraid I haven't the slightest sympathy with him, I know him too well.

I had a letter from Oscar Edwards but I don't think he had seen you then.

I quite understand how you feel about my going out but you must cheer up and I am always very lucky so I am sure to come through alright and when I do what a time we will have.

I know you must want me very much sometimes, I do you very often but I have to smile and look at my ring and generally cheer up. I do so love you and I know you aren't tired of hearing me say so. Don't forget the new address.

With all my love, Always your own Norman.

This is a picture of you and I in your drawing room when next I come home, time 11.30pm. Some rude person has put out the gas [light] so the figures are not very clear.

Oswestry
Thursday [5 July 1917 later that same day]

My own darling love,

Thank you very much for your nice long letters, evidently there are still one or two which have gone astray but I expect they will turn up later.

I am sorry to say I can't find out anything about my leave. We are moving to Swansea in a few days so I am afraid I shall not be able to let you know until the last minute. It is a pity but it can't be helped.

I have asked to get away on Friday night so unless you have a wire to the contrary will you meet the train at Snow Hill about 7.40 I think it is. I shall not be able to find out definitely until about 5pm tomorrow and that will just give me time to catch the train. [Leave didn't happen]

This is a very short letter but I am in a hurry to catch the post. I <u>do</u> hope I can come. With all my love, Always your own Norman.

[Writing from Oswestry but addressing his letter as from]
Singleton Park Camp
Sketty
near Swansea

5th July 1917

I went through my gas tests this morning. This is me:

My own darling love,

Thank you for your postcard this morning, I can't think why that packet hasn't reached you, but I will enquire this evening. It was only a few flowers but I thought you might like them. We are of course very busy getting ready for the move tomorrow and the above address is more accurate than the previous one I sent you.

I went to *The Glad Eye* last night, I had seen it twice before but enjoyed it as much as ever. I don't know whether you have seen it but it is absolutely a scream.

Those pictures I have I will bring home with me when next I come and perhaps you will look after them for me until we want them. They will do to go in a bedroom in our house.

You must not mind this letter being short, you can understand how we are pushed just at present. I will write a long letter on Sunday and let you know how we are.

I do wish I could come this weekend
With all my love. Always your own Norman.

I do love you angel xxxxx

2nd Lt. N.A.Wells
3/1st Herefordshire Regt.
attached 4th R.B. Kings Shropshire Light Infantry
Singleton Park Camp
Sketty
Swansea

[Saturday 7 July 1917]

My very own love,

I really feel that I have been neglecting you as regards letters during all this rush of moving and as I have a few minutes this morning before the train goes I am just sending a few lines to let you know you are not forgotten. You will see that we are being attached to the K.S.L.I. and the poor old Herefordshires are being disbanded, but we have all agreed to stick to our old regiment as long as we can so please address letters as above.

I am very sorry to leave here because it has such pleasant memories of you, but I hope in the future to come here with you as my wife and we can have a look at all the old spots.

Last night I went to some friends here and I had a long talk about you to a married lady I know very well. She is the wife of one of our fellows and has always wanted to meet you after all she has heard about you, so I hope you don't mind my discussing you to her – she is awfully nice. I told her you didn't want to get married just yet as you were afraid of growing old and she said she was quite the same before she got married but I am sure she would soon convert you if you met her, she has been so very happy since she risked it. Anyway we won't talk about it any more and you know I am always ready just when you are.

Could you copy the enclosed print, I thought it was rather saucy, and in watercolour and framed would look s'nice – particularly if made larger.

Please write as often as you can. I hope all the work is over for you now and that you are none the worse for it, you never say how you are. I am very fit but shall be glad when we are all settled.

With all my love, Always your own Norman.

Were you wanting me last night – Friday – about 10 o'clock, I did so want you and I wondered if it was one of our strange affairs. I am sure love makes us very close together even if we are a long way apart. Goodnight darling angel xxx

[The 3/1st Battalion was formed in Hereford in February 1915 as a depot/training unit and it had moved to Oswestry by September 1915. It was renamed the 1st Reserve Battalion in April 1916. As mentioned in Norman's letter of 7th July, his battalion merged with the 4th Reserve Battalion of the King's Shropshire Light Infantry at Swansea on 24 July 1917.]

1st Herefordshires
attached to 4th K.S.L.I.
Singleton Park Camp
Sketty
Swansea

Sunday [8 July 1917]

My very own love,

I have had no letter again this morning and am wondering why, as the Balance is surely over by now.

We arrived here safely at 5 o'clock yesterday and it is absolutely a topping camp. It is on a gentle slope down to the sea which is about a mile away and there are trees on either side. You know the Happy Valley at Llandudno, well this place is very like that. It poured with rain all night but the tents are nice and dry and I had a topping sleep. I dreamed a most strange dream last night. I dreamt that I had got engaged to someone else as well as you; who the other person was I don't know. I was in a fearful state about it but I knew you were there looking lovely and I kissed you several times so I woke up quite happy – only I wish I had you to kiss in reality.

I will let you know all about Swansea when I have had a look round and do write darling.
With all my love, Always your own Norman.

[For fun, Norman made up a 'Form for Engaged Ladies' for Amiel to complete, with an SAE addressed to himself at Singleton Camp, Swansea. The form gives a choice of address such as Dear, Dearest, Darling, and then offers other options such as I received/did not receive your letter/postcard/present of such and such date, and so on. There were obviously days when he was at a loose end!]

Sunday [the same day, 8 July 1917]

My own darling cherub,

Your lovely long letter has just arrived and although I have written to you once today I am starting another because I know it will be welcome to you. I am glad the roses turned up alright but it was a pity they got damaged – better luck next time. You mustn't expect me too much for next weekend because by what they tell me here leave is very difficult to get. You see I am not under the Herefords rule now but attached to the above and apparently the people here don't like us away on leave worse luck. All the same you know I am a pushing person and we will hope for the best. I do so want to see you – ever so much – it seems ages since I was home. I suppose it is having the change and extra work, but I am quite happy in every way as I know you are mine and I am yours for ever now. I am so glad I have that ring, you can't tell how it comforts me when I get lonely and I do get lonely sometimes even with all these jolly fellows around me.

It will be very nice for you at Dot's this weekend but if the weather is like it is here you won't get out much today. You mustn't let Dot's ideas alter yours, but I don't think they will, but always remember that each husband and wife live just their own lives together and cannot get help or anything from the advice of others. You will find that the best advice you will ever get will be from your Mother as she understands you best of all, even if you don't think it yourself. I have had many words with her you haven't thought of and I think such a lot of her for what she has said. You will be glad to know that my account is now £182 as it is pushing along and I hope before Xmas to have the £200 with luck – and it is all yours.

I do hope you will try to cheer up Mother a bit, she loves you very much and is so glad to have you. I mustn't tell you what she once said about you, you will think you ought to marry a duke instead of poor me and that would never do would it, but even if you are such an angel I do so want you and will honestly try to make your life even happier than it has been in the past.

Yes, you certainly haven't written much this week and you deserve two smacks – quite hard ones, but I expect all you will get will be umpteen kisses – and I hope soon. Re the candles and such like, can't you get them from your uncle as his stuff is so nice:

[He's referring here to Amiel's maternal Uncle Walter Witter who had set up Ickleford Industries in Ickleford, Hitchin, to train unemployed young men in metalwork. They made arts and crafts mirrors, candlesticks, trays and vases from copper, brass and pewter. For more information visit thewittercollection.co.uk]

and as regards the sketch and furnishing designs, you must decide those. You know heaps better than I do as to how to make a house pretty and I leave it all to you. I should like our dining room rather severe and old oak if poss; that very old clock of mine and some old pewter or brass about, the latter for preference, and the drawing room just a real lounge, with chairs big enough for the two of us to sit in one by a nice winter fire. What happy days to think about, when all this business is over.

We had a fine send off from Oswestry, crowds of people and all the big pots. The General shook hands with all the officers and wished us luck and the band played *Auld Lang Syne* and we all felt very miserable at being split up and leaving the old regiment. We had a good journey down and I walked as far as the shore last night with Boyce, but it was too late to see much of anything. From what the officers say it is a topping place but today it is awful. This is a sketch from where I am writing to you, taken from a large hut we use as a writing room.

View of bell tents in heavy rain through doorway of large hut.

Your sketch of your room was certainly true to life – but your people were there. If you had drawn it when they were not there it might have been different.

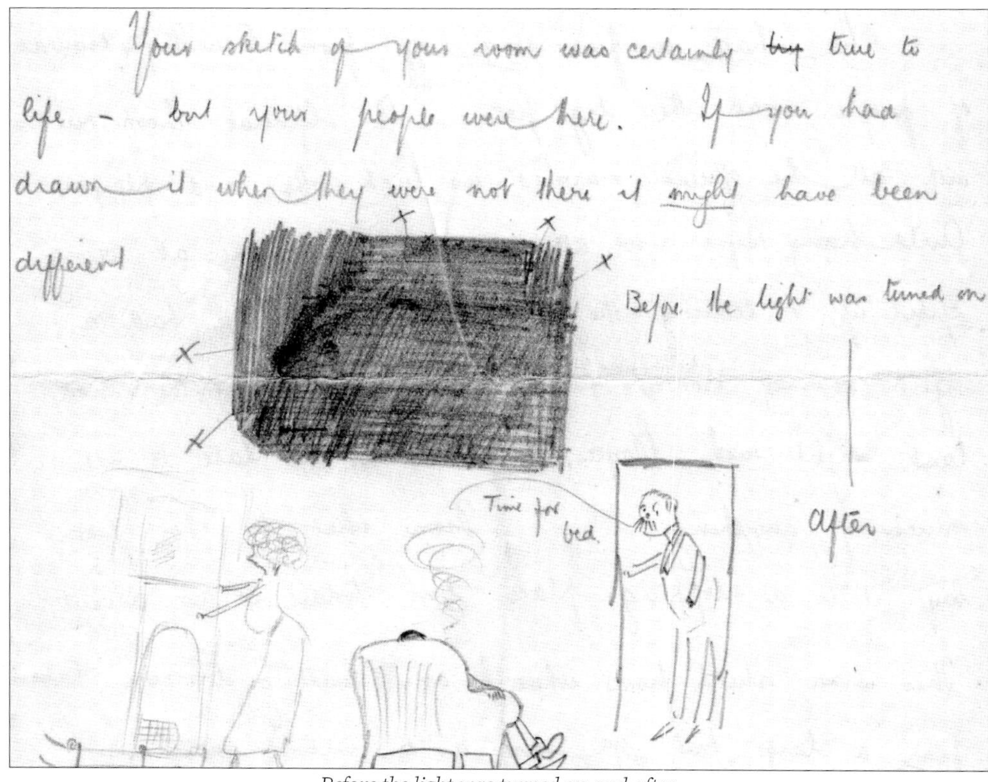

Your sketch of your room was certainly true to life – but your people were there. If you had drawn it when they were not there it might have been different

Before the light was turned on and after.

After all these many pages I shall expect a very long epistle.
With all my love, Always your Norman.

Extract from Amiel's Diary

Jul 11 Wednesday	*(no diary entries for 1-10 July)* N came at 5pm for 6 days. We went to Mrs W for tea. Walked up home through the park.
Jul 12 Thursday	N came to town at 12. Lunch at Patts. Intro N to . . . ? Theatre tickets for tomorrow. Bought me *Bing Girls are Here*. N came to Bank 4.30pm in flannels. He does look nice in white. Played tennis. After tea N back here. Music.
Jul 13 Friday	Met N at 12. He bought me pink carnations. Beauties. Went to Mrs Wells. Tea. *The Catch of the Season* very good song. N came home while Mr & Mrs W go on other tram. Fish and raspberries.
Jul 14 Saturday	Got out of Bank 1.20 N bought me carnations and chocs. Sutton Park. Glorious. Had ices. Then went on Windeley Pool [actually Wyndley Pool]. N rows toppingly. Boat rather damp. Tea at the Vesey. Sat watching "aeroplanes". Beautiful evening. M & F at Mrs Wells. Met Mr & Mrs Laibton. Great day altogether.
Jul 15 Sunday	N & I went to Mrs Wells for dinner. VEAL. Sleepy afternoon. Wet. Music. Tea. Came up home. Mr & Mrs Peckham. Lovely time while they played billiards. Music.
Jul 16 Monday	N met me at 12 o'clock. Coffee at Kardomah. Saw picture near Livery St. N brought me Turkish Delight. I didn't know he was there. Got out 4.30. A. Allie & Jack come for holiday. N & I called at shop & bought our <u>first</u> picture – girl's head & shoulders. Brought it up in Taxi. Tea. U. Fred here. Went to Elite Pictures. [Probably Elite Cinema on Soho Road, Handsworth, opened in 1913] Came back supper. N goes 9.30 tomorrow. I hate saying goodbye to him after such a lovely time.
Jul 17 Tuesday	N tried to ring up. No good. He went back to Swansea. Saw Mr & Mrs Wells for a little time.

Tuesday [17th July 1917]

My own darling Angel,

I am starting this in the train because I am feeling just a bit lonely and I felt I wanted to talk to you so much; you don't know how much I have enjoyed this leave – it has been the very best I have ever had and all through my little cherub. It is such a great comfort to me to feel so perfectly sure of you and of your love and to know that when I return you will be just the same loving sweetheart that I left last night.

I arrived at Hereford about 12 and went to see me old pal Shaw who is now discharged as I told you, he is very well and happy, he has been married about 12 months, and we had a long talk about things.

I went to Rogers to dinner where I had lamb, but had rather too much and felt awfully sleepy so I sat in the garden until 3.30 when I had a cup of tea and here I am in the train. I didn't see anyone special in Hereford but there was a topping pair of candlesticks in an antique shop. I didn't buy them but was very tempted.

I should just like to have a look at our picture now, I am so pleased with it and I hope now we have started you won't be afraid to get anything else you may see that you like. You can buy it and then ask me for the money, or if you would rather I will send you a cheque book and give you power to sign on my account. You needn't be a bit afraid to ask for the money as all there is is yours as I am always telling you.

Will you please thank your Mother for being so very kind to me; it is awfully good of her to be so sporty and let us have such times alone and I do appreciate it.

I hope I can get home and see you again very soon, it is all I look forward to and I often wonder whether other fellows feel so sad when they leave their cherubs behind, but I am sure a lot of them don't know love as we know it. Such love as we have cannot alter, however long we have to wait.

I must close now as the train wobbles so. Goodnight darling, you have all my love.
Always your own Norman.

Wednesday 7am
It has poured all night but I slept quite well and dreamed of you; but I can't remember details. Boyce is away on a course so I am all alone in my tent until Saturday. Owing to the rain all the spiders and black beetles in the camp have arrived in my tent so there have been many sudden deaths this morning.

Be sure you write soon. I do hope you are feeling better and will keep so, mind you tell me.
I will write again tomorrow xxxx
Your very own lover

Swansea
[Wednesday] 18th July 1917

My very own love,

Thank you very much for your nice long letter, I hardly expected one today but that made it all the nicer as it was a surprise. I was too late for the post last night but you will get my letter tomorrow I hope. It was a pity you couldn't get down to the station but they have been so very decent to you at the Bank that I can quite understand you don't want to ask for more. I would have called in at the Bank only I quite thought I could get through on the telephone but after trying umpteen times the lady informed me you were out of order – that is the telephone was.

Mother wanted to come to the station, at least she said she did, but as it always upsets her I said you would probably be there and got her to stay away. I am sure it was much better for her. I felt quite chirpy when I left home, I feel so very certain of my cherub that I can enter into my work much better now. I have dropped into a decent job for a few days but unfortunately it won't last long. I am giving final training to a draft warned for France. When they are warned they always turn the men over to an officer who polishes them up ready for the front. The fellow who has had charge of all the drafts in the past hasn't turned them out at all well so when I got back last night I was put in charge of the last one and it is very decent work. I make my own system of training and do just as I like with the men which is heaps better than ordinary parades and the last officer who had them treated them rottenly so they seem quite pleased. I hope to turn them out smarter than any other draft. Me if I do, pointing to:

Mind you look out for a nice pot-pourri bowl. A clisonné [sic] is very nice but unless you happen to spot one they are rather expensive. I shouldn't let the sun get to our picture too much until it has been revarnished but I know you know how to look after it.

I don't seem to have your mirror or lottery ticket. Which suit was it in?

Don't worry about last Saturday night, if you weren't feeling extra I can quite understand, but you should have said so – never mind dearest you are mine for ever and ever, and as you say – we shall be very happy.

I will finish this tomorrow as I have to get ready for dinner.

Thursday
I am afraid there is not much to say this morning. I had a topping night – slept dead from 11 to 6 and luckily it is much brighter this morning. I hope you had my letter yesterday – it is a bit slow here as Boyce is away on a course.

This afternoon we go down town on a special parade as the C.O. is presenting decorations to men of Swansea and the district, I will let you know all details in my next letter.

I do so love you angel and wish you were here as my very own – but someday – dearest.
With all my love. Always your own Norman

Swansea
[Friday] 20th July 1917

My own little sweetheart,

I didn't get a letter from you yesterday but am hoping one will come sometime today.

We had quite a decent time yesterday down in Swansea. We marched down to the chief park at 2 o'clock and the C.O. presented medals to a lot of South Wales men. Some of them had done awfully brave things, and a lot were wounded. The worst part was when relatives of a dead man had to receive the medals. There were thousands of people in the streets and in the park to watch all the business and I wish you could have been among them. In the evening before dinner I walked down to the shore with two more fellows and everything looked extra. There were heaps of people bathing and the sky and sea were a very deep blue. This is a topping place, quite the best I have ever been in and it only wants you here to be near me to make it perfect.

[This was a fête and gala held in Victoria Park, Swansea, where the Guildhall with the Brangwyn panels has since been built. The fête was in aid of the Provincial Police Orphanage. Lieutenant Colonel Symons-Taylor presented military medals to several soldiers for bravery in the battlefield. He could sympathise with the parents who received a medal on behalf of their son who had since died as his own son had been decorated and had also died.]

If I am not warned for draft in the next fortnight I am most likely going to Oswestry for a month. I shall not be in the camp but at a private billet in the town and I am sure I shall like it particularly if I can get a weekend with you. Do you think your Father would let you go to Whittington for a weekend while I am in Oswestry? I am sure a little change would do both you and your Mother good if your Father could spare you both from Saturday to a Monday. You could get off a few hours from the Bank or feel bad.

We have had a nice day today but I was hoping to get a letter. We went out into the sandhills on the beach and cooked our dinners and had great attacks etc.
Now do be quick and write as I want so much to get a letter. I do wish you were here it is lovely weather but 'orrid 'ot.

Goodnight darling I do love you.
With all my love. Always your own Norman.

Singleton Camp
Swansea
[Saturday] 21st July 1917

My own darling,

I was so pleased to get 1 1/2 letters from you today but the half one was short although welcome as I hadn't heard since Wednesday. I am Orderly Officer today so am staying in camp of course; I don't mind very much as I have spent most of the day either under the shower bath or sitting in a deck chair watching the ships through some glasses. Boyce returned this afternoon but is rather upset as he has lost his luggage en route and is now frantically racing between here and the station to try to find it.

It was so nice of you to write as you did and tell me all your thoughts. You need never be afraid of what you put as it is all very sacred to me and as we are so certain of each other we needn't be shy of expressing our love. I can quite understand that you feel jealous sometimes; I do most fearfully although now I am so sure of your love and you, I think I am much better than when first I loved you. Of course I couldn't bear to think that anyone shared a little bit of your love for me, love for parents is quite a different matter, but I know you so well and trust in your goodness so that I am sure such a thing is impossible. You are such an angel to all other girls.

Now do be careful darling with that cold, and be sure you let me know how it is, because they are very nasty to get in the summer. I am glad you have been home as they would be very glad to see you I know.

It is very decent of Sid Easy to say such nice things, but he doesn't really know me at all, does he? Anyway I shall try to make you very happy and I think you feel this in yourself because you didn't seem nearly so frightened of me, and I am sure there is no reason to be. If you think I seem hard sometimes don't be upset because it gets a habit in the army although I am sure the men don't think I am so very bad. All the same one must keep one's position and I am responsible that certain work is done and therefore I see it is done so I suppose a little abruptness gets a habit. It soon wears off though dear with you near me, and as you know I wouldn't harm you in the least, and I shall always take great care of you and your love, and I can't do more can I?

Goodnight my darling, I do love you and you have all my love.
Your very loving Norman.

Extract from Amiel's Diary

Jul 18 Wednesday	Busy day balancing ledgers. At first sight 1/– wrong. Balanced 7pm. Wish N were here.
Jul 19 Thursday	Letter from N. Saw Mr & Mrs W in the park & went out to them for a few minutes.
Jul 20 Friday	Letter from N. Had tea with Dot. Singing lesson. Came home more music.
Jul 21 Saturday	Letter from N. Bought wee hat shape & straw. Made hat all afternoon. Went up to tennis 7.30 Bought photo prints. Jolly time at tennis. Miss Omand sang *Coming Home.* "Gut." Aunty Allie, M & Jack went to Edgbaston.
Jul 22 Sunday	No letter. Up 12. Day in gardens. A. Allie & Jack enjoyed it. Gladys S. sent me a hanky. First attempt at printing photos. 'Trés bon.' Singing until 1130. Dinner, Tea & Supper in the garden. [It must have been a hot day.]

Swansea
[Monday] 23rd July 1917

My very own darling,

No letter today or yesterday so I do hope to have one tomorrow. You said in your last you were going to write every day.

It is the greatest wonder that I am not in France tonight. A draft left this morning and I asked to go over with them. It would have been a fine experience as I should have gone right up into the line with them and then returned here in a week or two; they promised to send me but discovered later that it would have interfered with my course at Oswestry so another lucky fellow went.

I don't know whether I told you but one of my old pals from the Buffs arrived here on Friday. Yesterday we both went to Mumbles and walked to Langham Bay [Langland Bay]. I did wish you could have seen it with us, it is absolutely lovely and quite as pretty as Devonshire, all rocks and rough sea. Do you know what I thought, I don't know whether I ought to tell you, but I'll whisper – 'Just the place for our honeymoon.'

I have heard nothing about the weekend but I shall do my best to come on Saturday although I am afraid it may be too late to see you until Sunday.

Now do write very soon please, if you haven't already done so.
With all my love. Always your own Norman.

Amiel on grass bank.

Amiel with apple blossom.

Swansea
[Tuesday] 24th July 1917

My own darling love,

I have just posted a letter to you, but now find that two very nice long letters have come from you so I thought I would just send another little one to you.

I think the coloured photos are <u>extra</u> particularly the one with the apple blossom and it does so bring back those happy days. You have done them awfully well and I am very proud of such a brainy little cherub, I wish I could do things like that, but as you are me and I am you it comes to the same thing. [We still have a locket on a chain that Amiel's mother wore in which there are two hand coloured photos of Amiel, one with the apple blossom, both taken at the time of their engagement in Oswestry.]

I am sorry you don't think you can get a weekend at Oswestry but never mind I must try to come and see you as often as possible, that is if I go there.

Last night I went down to Swansea but felt so fearfully tired I came back and went straight to bed about 9 o'clock; I think I must have been caught by the sun a bit, it was fearfully hot here in the afternoon. I feel quite alright again today and hope to go with Boyce to Mumbles tonight. He hasn't found his luggage yet, it is most awkward for him and he sends umpteen telegrams per day in search of it. I will write again tomorrow and a longer letter. I do so love you and hope to see you soon.

With all my love. Always your very own Norman.

Extract from Amiel's Diary

Jul 23 Monday	Letter from N. Home from Bank 5pm. Called for F. Ironed, printed & painted photos. Bed.
Jul 24 Tuesday	–
Jul 25 Wednesday	Letter from N. Balanced ledgers till 9.45 Tea at Patts with 2 Pilchers & P. Boyton. Some fun.
Jul 26 Thursday	Letter from N. After Bank called at Griffins. Brought Cay home. Auntie Allie & Jack went home 4.30. M went to Mrs Gough. F to tennis. Wrote to N & Madge. Read.
Jul 27 Friday	Madge brought *Allies* photos to Bank. 'Bon.' Wet at night. Turned out sitting room with M. Singing. Bed.
Jul 28 Saturday	Letter from N. N came at 1.35. Dinner with Mrs Wells. Walked round to club. Came home. Had tea in garden. M & F at tennis. Went round VX. [Villa Cross Picture House, built 1913] Came back. I hate N leaving me at night. Supper. Bed.
Jul 29 Sunday	[No diary entries until 6th August]

[There's also a gap in the letters from Norman during this time until 7th August.]

Extract from Amiel's Diary

Aug 6 Monday	Bank Holiday. N went to Oswestry 4pm. I walked to Dots. Music. Jolly time. Went for ice cream. Croquet. Supper. Music. I wrote to N. Serious moon.
Aug 7 Tuesday	Letter from N. Mr & Mrs Wayne came, also Mr & Mrs Wells. Billiards. Music. Dot stayed night.
Aug 8 Wednesday	L from N. Left Bank at 8pm. Hot bath. Bed.
Aug 9 Thursday	L from N.
Aug 10 Friday	L from N. Went to Masons about photos.
Aug 11 Saturday	N came into Bank. Had lunch at Barrow with Marg Nock. [Probably refers to the restaurant at upmarket Barrow's Stores in Birmingham city centre.] Met N. Went to Art Gallery. Tea at Mrs Wells. Walked round to tennis club.
	[No entries till 18th August]
Aug 18 Saturday	N home.
	[No entries till 1st September]

[Not many letters have been found for August and none for September. Norman mentioned in an earlier letter from Swansea that he was going on a course in Oswestry sometime in August, so I have assumed that the horse-riding course described in the letters that follow, date from this period.

Amiel's diary doesn't have many entries to help with the detail. In September she goes on holiday with Dot, joining their parents in Aberystwyth. Although there are no surviving letters from Norman until October, Amiel refers in her diary to having received several during this period.]

Tuesday [possibly 7th August]
26 Ferrers Road,
Oswestry

My own darling Love,

You remember that tale about the princess and the bean, how she could feel the bean through any number of cushions, well it is easily explained, she couldn't put it down to blue blood as the tale says, but she had just returned from a riding school. By this you will understand the value of this letter as it means being quite a martyr to sit down and write. I seriously thought of eating my tea off the mantlepiece but my landlady might have thought it odd.

The first day here has been very enjoyable. We had physical drill from 7-7.30, lecture 9.30-10.30, and 11 to 12.30 drill. All afternoon we have been riding and I do this each afternoon, that is I take it if we aren't casualties or all worn away. If I should come home on Saturday you won't know me I shall be that altered.

But seriously, a riding school isn't quite like sitting on a horse in a field at a farm as I used to do at Hereford. We have an enclosed ring in the centre of a field and it is ever so small, and tear round this and do all sorts of strange feats while the major tickles up your horse with a long whip much to your and the horse's delight.

There are 10 officers here and apparently I am the junior. I have another fellow sharing my sitting room, a captain, and he is an awfully nice chap, married and quite a good sort.

Last night I called on some friends of mine and they were very pleased to see me. You remember me mentioning a nice chap named Knapp, he has now got the Military Cross and I am very glad, he is a good soldier.

I can't find anything about the weekend, but live in hope, I shall come if I can as you know.

I had a feather bed last night but hardly slept at all, why I don't know; I have had it altered to a very hard one and after such a strenuous day I am sure I shall be alright.

Be sure you write soon, and just in case you don't know (???) – I do so love you darling.
With all my love, Always your very own Norman.

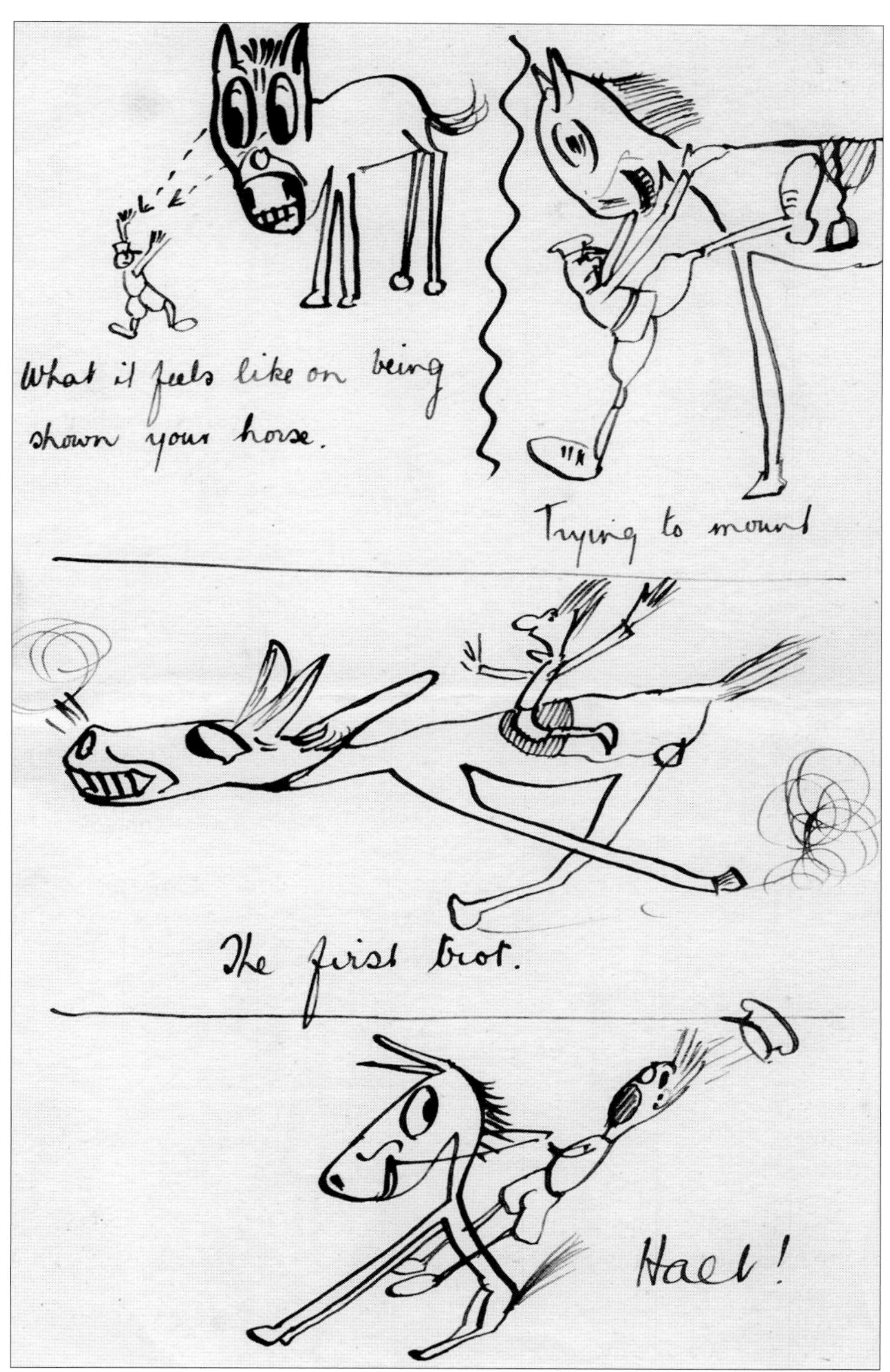
What it feels like on being shown your horse.
Trying to mount
The first trot.
Halt!

In the ring
Landlady.
Have you enjoyed the ride Sir!
Home!!

[The start of this next letter is missing but Norman is still on his horse riding course, which I have assumed took place in August.]

. . . big enough for us to long for marriage.

They must be having a warm time in France just now, [he may well be referring here to the third battle of Ypres which started on 31st July] and I am just a bit envious, but I know I mustn't want to go out as there is you to think of now besides Mother. You don't know how glad I am that I have got you all for myself, it means so much to me but I shall be so glad when all this business is over so that I can come back to you for ever.

Last weekend was the best I have ever had with you, I felt so sure of you and knew you did of me. I must go now to work and will finish this later.

Evening.
I have just returned from an afternoon's riding and I must say it has been the limit. Round and round the ring all the time and the horse I got this afternoon was particularly annoyed at something. We have to change them each day so that we get used to all kinds. We have to ride with arms folded, touching one toe and many other strange things. This is how I feel.

I must go now. I find I shall have to leave home Sunday afternoon, but I think I had better come. One evening with my angel is worth a lot. Goodnight, darling.
With all my love, Always your own Norman.

From L-R, Dot, Amiel and Mrs Robins on holiday near Aberystwyth.

Extract from Amiel's Diary

Sep 1 Saturday	Stayed with Dot while F & M & Mr & Mrs Wayne [Dot's parents] went to Aberystwyth.
Sep 5 Wednesday	I met Dot. Caught train to Aberystwyth. Lost purse. Got to Aber 6.30pm. Dinner. Walked along prom. Music. Bed.
	[No entries while on holiday in Aberystwyth]
Sep 15 Saturday	Dot, F & I came back from Aberystwyth. Mr Rednall came at the same time. Shopped at night.
Sep 16 Sunday	L from N. Got up 12. Cooked dinner. Made scones. Walked to Mrs Wells. Still away.
Sep 17 Monday	L from N. Started work again.
Sep 18 Tuesday	L from N.
Sep 19 Wednesday	–
Sep 20 Thursday	Wire from N. Leaves for Egypt. New Street 4.15. Taxied to Mrs Wells. Tea. Allies at Churchfields, West Bromwich. F at Wayne's. It's good to have N again. Came home in van – also Ted Wall & F. Wright – none so nice as <u>my</u> Bunny.
Sep 21 Friday	Saw N 11 o'clock. Lunch with him at 12. Came down at 4. Tea at home. Quiet evening. At last he's starting to love me properly. I am glad.
Sep 22 Saturday	Allies at Monyhull 6.30pm. [Monyhull, Kings Norton, was a military hospital that saw several thousand wounded and shell shocked soldiers in WW1].
Sep 23 Sunday	[No entries till 6th October]

PART III:

ABROAD AT LAST

Extract from Amiel's Diary

Oct 6 Saturday	YWCA Saltley (didn't go) Bought N vest pocket Kodak. Saw F & Edwards in village. N bought me Kunzle's chocs. Went to Mrs W for tea. Walked round the wood. Came back. N stayed the night.
Oct 7 Sunday	Stayed night at Mrs Wells. Went to St Michael's church. Very happy.
Oct 8 Monday	Allies at Harborne 7pm (didn't go).
Oct 9 Tuesday	N goes to Southampton.

[The vest pocket Kodak camera that Amiel gave Norman was very popular with soldiers as it was small enough to carry easily and they could take photographs of their experiences. Norman refers to this in his letter of 15th December.]

Southampton
Tuesday [9th Oct 1917]

My own beloved,

I don't feel much like writing a letter but I want to tell you that I am very nearly at S'hampton. I am very glad that this morning is over, I think it has been one of the worst ordeals of my life. I am sorry I behaved so foolishly, I really can't hide my feelings like some people, I suppose it is because I am not so brave, but I know you understand and so I don't mind very much because as you say I am only a baby after all. I can't say very much now darling, in a few days I shall be more normal but just remember that as long as I live I am yours body and soul. Try to forgive my weaknesses, because they were nothing more, and no harm was meant to you as you know. I shall always try to be a good husband to you and every night I shall pray that you are safe and well and that our love continues as strong as it is now.

Do what you can for Mother darling, it is very hard for her because she is so much older. Always remember I am yours to the very end. I shall write just when I can so if you don't get another letter you will know I am going by sea all the way.

With all my love. Yours for ever, Norman
I will write to your Mother soon.

The Waverley Hotel, [hotel headed writing paper]
Bournemouth
Wed 10th October 1917

My darling,

I am glad to say my tummy is nearly well now and I have had a very fine breakfast.

After I wrote you yesterday I decided to come here as Southampton didn't seem very lively and I felt I wanted to have someone to talk to. I got here about 5pm and went to my aunt's causing great rejoicing and surprise as you can guess. They hadn't seen me for years and they didn't know me at first. Oh my love, you can't imagine what my feelings were when you left me on the station. I was so glad you went before the train, it made it so much easier for me but all the same it was quite hard enough. I am a fearful coward at seeing people in trouble and seeing Mother and Father and yours too and also you my darling nearly did for me as you know. I know you quite understand and don't think me silly but I wish I could be braver. Anyway you know now how much I do love you and it is for ever. But I mustn't make you sad although it helps me when I tell you all.

After going to my aunt's I went to the Winter Gardens and there was a topping show on. The band was extra and the Russian Ballet was there. Also a troupe called 'The Allies' but not like the originals.

There was only one thing the whole evening to upset things and that was a girl singing 'Burlington Bertie' and it started all the old tummy pains and I thought I should have to go out but I stuck it well, oh, but it was horrible while it lasted.

This hotel is topping, huge feeds and a lovely bed. I was very fortunate in meeting a topping chap in the hotel and things passed very merrily, but I dreamed of my angel all the night.

I shall try to find out my next address for you and will put it in this letter.

Try to make the best of all this trouble love, and remember what I promised you – I am yours for ever and ever but I don't know why I keep telling you this as I know you are as sure of it as I am.

I don't know when I shall have a letter from you or you from me again but God bless you always love and keep you safe for me.

With all my love, Your loving sweetheart, Norman.

I am sending the above letter as I thought you would like it although we are not sailing for a few days. I don't know what I shall be doing, I expect I shall have to return to Swansea so don't write anywhere until you hear from me again. I am having a good time here, all my pals are with me except Mogridge and he seems to have got lost en route. I will write tomorrow with any news there is but I am quite safe for a few days.

xxxxxxx Goodnight darling, Norman.

If you see anyone like this it is Moggy and he is lost so tell him where we are.

Extract from Amiel's Diary

Oct 10 Wednesday	Balanced ledgers. Went to Mrs W. Had wire from N. Not gone yet.
Oct 11 Thursday	N came back again. Rang up from Snow Hill. Great excitement. Tea at Mrs Wells, rehearsal at Griffins. N went home, I followed.
Oct 12 Friday	Lunch at Co-op. Tea at home. Cosy time in dining room. Went to Mrs Wells for the night.
Oct 13 Saturday	Small Heath 7pm. Topping show. N off again to S'hampton.

Extract from Norman's Diary
[This was copied by hand by Amiel from the original.]

Oct 11 Thursday	*Reported at Southampton but was not wanted so returned home.*
Oct 14 Sunday	*Left Southampton but had to turn back owing to Submarines.*
Oct 15 Monday	*Sailed from Southampton on SS Queen Alexandria.*
Oct 16 Tuesday	*Arrived at Cherbourg.*
Oct 17 Wednesday	*Arrived at St Germain.*

Heathfield Commercial Hotel (Mrs M A Lines, Proprietress)
West Park Road
Southampton

Sunday [14th Oct 1917]

My own beloved,

I really don't feel much like letter writing. I haven't got settled down yet but don't think you are being forgotten. When I got to Reading I met Mogridge and we travelled down together arriving here about 3. When we reported at the embarkation office we were told that we should not sail until today, so we found the above hotel after a lot of trouble as everywhere was so crowded, but we are very comfortable. I expect by the time you read this I shall be in France and I shall be wanting you very very much. Yesterday morning I went off very cheerfully but I didn't feel it inside and my tummy was nasty again, all the same I feel heaps more sure of you even after just that little time again together and I am very glad I came. I am quite sure of my love for you and yours for me so we have nothing to worry about but just to be patient until we can be together again. In a few days I shall be more settled and can write better then perhaps. I do love you darling for ever and ever.

Always your very own, Norman.
I had your letter from the post office and was very cheered by it.

Extract from Amiel's Diary

Oct 16 Tuesday	Saw Mrs Wells after Bank.
Oct 17 Wednesday	L from N.
Oct 18 Thursday	L from Mrs Wells. Cable from N. [Allies at] Uffculme 7.30pm [Moseley]. Rotten show. Ted, Ethel's boy home wounded.
Oct 19 Friday	2 PPCS & L from N. [picture postcards] F's birthday. Bought him lined gloves. Saw *General Post.* [A comedy in 3 acts by J.E.Harold Terry, which reflects the amazing social change wrought by the war.]
Oct 20 Saturday	–
Oct 21 Sunday	3 to N [3rd letter written to N while on active service]
Oct 22 Monday	PC from N.
Oct 23 Tuesday	–
Oct 24 Wednesday	4 to N.
Oct 25 Thursday	2 letters from N. 4,5.
Oct 26 Friday	–
Oct 27 Saturday	Maxstoke Castle 7pm. Rode in Mr Hales' Daimler. Topping car. [Maxstoke Castle is 3 miles outside Coleshill, Warwickshire, and in private hands.]
Oct 28 Sunday	–
Oct 29 Monday	–
Oct 30 Tuesday	Allies Selly Oak.
Oct 31 Wednesday	–

A rest camp in France
Tuesday [16 Oct 1917]

My very own love,

We left England at dusk last night and hung about for a few hours until we picked up a destroyer who was to escort us over. We shot off at full speed and got over to France about midnight. The crossing was fairly smooth although the boat was so small it rolled a good deal. It was bitterly cold on deck but I got a blanket and a muffler and a comfortable place near the funnel and tried to be happy. I am sorry to say I did not feel very well on the voyage, we got in a nasty squall about 10 o'clock and that settled me. I was bad for about 5 minutes but was soon alright again and able to get into a cabin. We anchored off the harbour and I then went to sleep until

6 o'clock this morning. I then had a fine breakfast on board of ham and eggs and thoroughly enjoyed it. We disembarked about 8 o'clock and as I am Adjutant of the boat and trains and voyage in general I had plenty to do to keep me busy. The camp is about 4 miles from the docks but I thought in consideration of my position I would ride up on a tram. I had a fearful job to be understood and the people in the tram were only too anxious to be a help to me and they talked away 15 to the dozen all in French of course. I managed to make the conductress understand at last and arrived here safely. We are in very nice huts and all most comfortable but I expect we shall be pushing on south tomorrow. Oh my dear I do wish you could be with me, you have no idea how interesting and lovely everything is here. The French soldiers in their blue coats and red breeches, the market women in lace hats and sabots filled with hay and very wide short skirts.

We are in camp in the grounds of a most lovely chateau which is now a hospital. [This is probably at Tourlaville which was No.1 Rest Camp with a chateau nearby.] It is quite the sort we see in fairy stories, all gabled towers and curly staircases and surrounded by tall palm trees and a long sort of plumy grass. It has several large lakes and numerous cascades and waterfalls whilst in the courtyard are three fine fountains, just single jets coming from the ground in little ponds.

This is an idea of what the towers are like.

The camp is near an old village all stone cottages and an old cross. There is a fine old church and a ruin of the old chateau which I hope to explore soon. The port itself is a big sleepy sort of place, very few decent shops and very few people about. There is the usual cathedral on a hill in the centre and I am glad to say the weather is much warmer here. Will you please let Mother and Father know I have written and read them what you like of this letter. I am very fit and am really enjoying this. There is a spirit of adventure in this that I have never felt before but through it all dearest you are before me and I feel I am doing this for you. Never fear that my love will alter, I do miss you and want you but know you will be just the same when I return for I do love you darling.

With all my love, Always your own Norman.
I wired Mother that I arrived safely and I hope you heard from them.

[The next few lines were written on a French picture postcard of an artist's pen drawing of a girl with a dog, postmarked 'Army Post Office' and written 'On Active Service']

17th October 1917

We are leaving our rest camp today for the south. I have had a fine time here and am sending a letter home with all news. I will write you as well and will post at our first stopping place.
Much love, N.

In the train.
France
18th October 1917 [postmarked 22nd Oct 1917]

My very own beloved,

I have not been able to write the last day or two as I have had such a lot to see to, I have been buzzing about from early until late, and I am rather uncertain when I shall post this as we are moving towards Italy and Army Post Offices are scarce but in any case I hope you get this.

I have been longing for a letter from you it seems such a while since I left you, it must be all these adventures I have been having, and I do hope you have written to Taranto because I may be there some time. Anyway when I get to Egypt I shall expect such nice long ones and those will make up for it.

To continue from my last letter. We duly arrived in France as you know and after a good feed a fellow and myself went into the town to see what was on. From the camp we went by an electric tram, which apparently seems to run away with itself and then stop suddenly, so much so that I noticed the driver was strapped to the driving apparatus to save him from being thrown out. All the drivers and conductors are women, but not a bit like ours, they carry on what is apparently a fierce argument the whole time, in fact to a stranger everyone seems to be quarrelling in France but I understand that is merely their manner. We explored the cathedral, it is massive but very poor inside.

We then went to an hotel where no English was spoken and had dinner. I did wish you could have been there, it was quite an education. We had some lovely soup but served up with huge pieces of bread in it, in fact this course alone was a meal but I went easy with it. Next we had lemon sole in white wine which was extra. As an entree they served cauliflower all on its own and the natives helped themselves to a huge plateful piled up high – they have a great partiality for cauliflower. Next we had hot roast horse and with bread only, it is awfully nice if you can get over the idea of it, my pal couldn't tackle it but I found the flavour topping but it was just a bit coarse and tough. After this we had a beautiful salad, followed by omelette and rum which is really first rate. We finished with cheese and a lot of it. Unfortunately we are forbidden to drink water out here unless supplied by the army, so it is rather awkward. We had to hurry back to our tram as the last one went at 8.15. When we got off it we had to walk about a mile to the camp and of course we got lost. We wandered for about an hour and had to go right back and start again.

Next morning I had to go into the town on Army business and was there all day so I didn't have much chance of sightseeing. I have most thrilling times with my French as hardly anyone seems to know English, but I am getting on all right. You hear a lot about French girls being pretty. They are not a bit, but they certainly look very smart when they are all dressed up. Their style is good but they make up fearfully and I didn't see one that would attract me in the least, not that I wanted one and I expect I shall wait for a long time before I see one like my cherub. Oh I do miss you darling and do so want you, but I have to look ahead and not behind as I get awfully lonely. I know you will wait for me for ever and that is a great comfort to me – and I have my ring and that helps ever so much. I must stop for a bit as we are going to have breakfast. I hope you can read this as the train wobbles fearfully.

I have just cut my finger so my writing will be much worse so please excuse.
We are now nearing the south of France and it is getting much warmer and the scenery is great. We left our camp last night at 9 o'clock – travelled all night. I am in a very comfortable carriage with one other and we are getting good food.

We have just passed a lot of Turkish prisoners, they look very happy here. The country here is fine and most interesting and I will write again as soon as I get a chance. I do so want you and love you more each day and do hope I come back to you soon. God bless you always love – goodnight darling.
Always your very own, Norman.

Extracts from Norman's Diary

Oct 19 Friday	*Arrived at St Germain.*
Oct 21 Sunday	*Passed through Alps and arrived Firenza.*
Oct 25 Thursday	*Arrived Taranto Italy.*
Oct 27 Saturday	*Sailed from Taranto.*

No.2 Rest Camp
S.E. France
19th Oct 1917 [postmarked 22nd Oct 1917]

Beloved,

I have just posted a long newsy letter tonight to you and another to Mother but am feeling just a wee bit lonely and I feel as though I just want your arms round me for one minute to put me right so I am sending this short note to you to cheer me up.

It seems such a long long time since I left you, but I really have had a good time. Active service is very superior to England, I feel that I am really doing something and not slacking but it is such a long long way from you darling. All the same you know as well as I do that we are really each other's for all time now, so distance doesn't matter much does it, only a little time together is so very nice.

I will write to your Mother and Father as soon as I get a chance, but my job as Adjutant means work 23 99/100ths of the day and the rest of the time I really must eat etc. I haven't had a chance for a shave today so you can tell how much I am doing. It was a case of a line to you or a shave so you see what trouble you are getting me into.

I must go to bed now darling. Do your best for Mother please, and try to keep cheerful and well yourself. I shall be with you again soon I hope and then for keeps. Goodnight my own. I do love you – the real true love that won't alter.

Give just a bit of my love to your Mother and Father, you have all I have in my heart.
Always your very very own Norman.

Italia
Sunday 21 Oct 1917

My very own love,

Please read this to my M & F. (My, Aint' it 'orrid 'ot.) I expect you will be surprised to hear this but it is really hot, we have caught up summer and with a vengeance. When last I wrote to you we were in France but now we have been through what I expect will have been the very best part of our journey, that is right through the Alps. People talk about Wales and those places but I have never seen anything so marvellous as this in my life. I was up early this morning, about 5am and the temperature was 25 degrees below freezing so you can tell it was a bit chilly. But although the temperature was so low and deep snow all round, we were 2000 feet up, it was warm enough to be without a coat, owing to the extreme dryness of the air. We had a fine breakfast of omelettes, the chief dish in this part, and very dark honey. After that I went out and watched the sunlight creeping down the glaciers and between the peaks of the Alps. I can't attempt to describe the scenery, it is so wonderful and compressed. I have never seen torrents like these, or valleys, or such mountains; and perched on the most awful peaks are the monasteries of the many orders round here. When once a man has climbed up there no wonder he never wants to get down again, it would be too much to do twice in a lifetime. On one peak 1100 feet high we saw a house right on the summit, far above the midsummer snow line, and were told that it was the home of a recluse, but how he gets any food I can't tell. We passed through this sort of scenery for 10 hours, groves of maize, olives, lemons, oranges, and Indian corn, and are just having a rest and some tea. We are now near a big town in Italy and in the distance we can still see the snow topped peaks of the Alps. This is what it looks like drawn from where I am.

I don't know the name of the very high peak but it must be something famous. My Italian at present is very limited but I shall progress in time. We had quite forgotten the war until today and we have seen heaps of aeroplanes, and very good ones they seem, particularly for speed. The Italian soldiers are real chocolate ones, [referring to Shaw's *Arms and the Man* perhaps?] worse than Serbs, and two lieutenants have been trying to make me understand something with heaps of bows and smiles and salutes. They all look like budding Napoleons in their dress and are even more quaint than the Alpins who come from this part but the other side of the border of course.

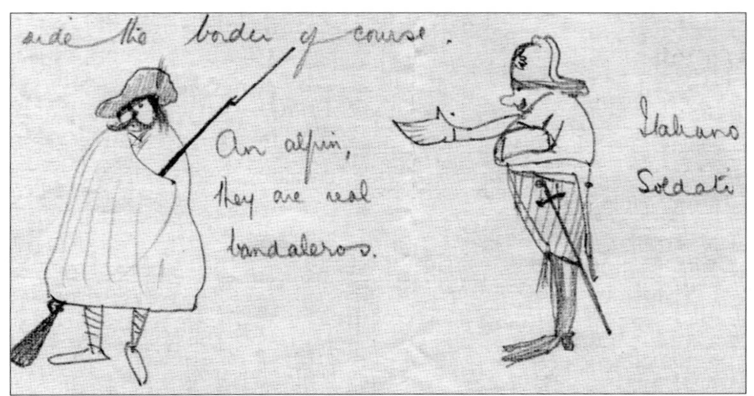

An Alpin, they are real bandaleros. and an 'Italiano Soldato'.

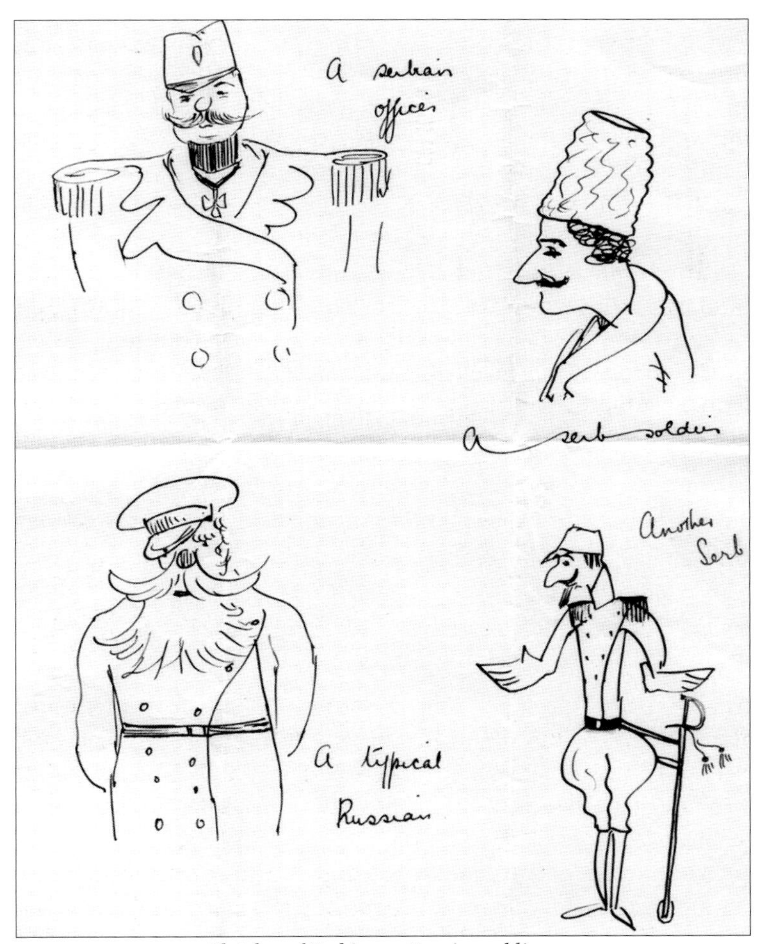

Sketches of Serbian or Russian soldiers.

I don't know how my letters and postcards are arriving but I hope you get them all because I know you must be worrying if you don't. Today is Sunday but I can't realise it a bit. Who would have thought that in a fortnight I should have left you and be in the land of perpetual sun, not a cloud in the sky, and such a sky as you never saw except in a Turner picture. The colours are so vivid that they look unreal to an Englishman but I am here alright.

The next is for you alone.
Now dearie don't worry about me. I never felt better in my life, my love for you gets more every day and I do want you although I am making myself be resigned to my lot. I am very happy I have heaps of rattling fine men with me and I am going out to do the best bit of work I have ever done. When I am back I shall be glad I have been allowed to help to get peace for you and all at home – it will be worth it darling. I had the courage to look at your photo today for the first time. I have 3 with me. I have no fears of your love altering and I know mine never will – think of me each night as I do of you and God bless you always my own.

Your ever loving sweetheart, Norman.

No 9 Rest Camp [Taranto, Italy]
[postmarked 26th Oct 1917]

My own beloved,

I have just a few minutes before I go to my little bed and sleep after a very hard day's work. I honestly haven't had time for a breather since 6 this morning but I don't mind a little bit as it gives me plenty to think about and I can't be homesick when I have such a lot to do. I have got a decent little office here and outside there is a gramophone playing away as I write this, it has just been on the *Oh Oh Oceans of joy for you* and it did remind me of those dear old happy days which seem such a long way off. Italy is all very well, blue skies and seas and palm trees may be nice in books and pictures, but when evening comes I always seem to see you at home or singing to me and the thousands of miles we are apart seem very small and you at this moment are very near to me. You can't tell what a great comfort it is to me to be so sure of your love and to know that you will always be true.

I don't know when we shall leave here probably in a day or two but I hope to be able to write again before I do go. You mustn't think I am depressed in this letter because I am not and I really feel very fit and happy, but I do wish I could have an hour with you tonight and I know you do. Some more work has just come in so I must now close and I thought I was going to bed. I do love you angel and I am sure you know it. I will try to write a long letter tomorrow.

With all my love. Always your very own Norman.
Goodnight love – God bless you.

No. 9 Rest Camp
27th Oct 1917

My very own darling,

I have just heard that I am to sail in the morning, at least we shall go on the boat so this will be the last letter I can write for some days. As soon as I get to Egypt I will cable home to say I am safe and will you please tell Mother I am sailing as I haven't time to write home again today. I have been having a very busy time and am afraid shall continue so for a while at any rate but you can always be sure that your sweet face is with me and guiding me to do what I think is right. I shall come back soon never fear and whilst I am onboard I will write you a very long letter. I shall be glad to get the journey over, it has seemed a very long one but in a few days it will be over. I must go now dearest to bed as I have to be up at 5 tomorrow.

Goodnight dearest I love you more than I can tell and I shall always be true never fear. With all my love, Always your very own Norman.

Onboard ship from Taranto, Italy to Alexandria, Egypt.

Onboard ship from Taranto, Italy to Alexandria, Egypt.

[With stalemate on the Western Front it was thought that a campaign in Palestine would divert the German forces to the east. In terms of forces deployed, the war in Palestine became the second largest after the Western Front. Norman arrives in Egypt and the start of a long trail to Hebron and beyond.]

1st Herefordshires
53rd Division
E.E.F. [Egyptian Expeditionary Force]

Friday 2nd Nov 1917

My own darling,

I don't know when you will get this letter as I know the post is very erratic from here and I am miles away from all western ideas now.

We reached Alexandria yesterday and I had a most enjoyable time there. There is so much to say and all is so wonderful I don't quite know where to start. When you get to Alex the port is very like any English docks but as soon as you land there seems to be a sharp line drawn and the west becomes east straight away. The streets are full of camels, asses, veiled women and all the strange costume of the east. The women are all wrapped up and you cannot see more than their eyes, which makes them seem rather mysterious. (We have just stopped at the place where Wolseley defeated the Sudanese). [Tel El Kebir?] The women are almost white, that is the bit you see of them, but the men are all colours. The better class wear fezzes and a sort of nightshirt down to their ankles, and they have sandals on. The poorer classes wear turbans or skull caps and large baggy breeches, what we call harem skirts and everyone carries an umbrella to keep the sun off. All the men and women have bangles in profusion round their ankles and all their money, which has a hole in the centre, they wear in their ears, noses or round their necks.

All the advertisements are in Arabic and you can pick out Bovril, Black and White etc by the pictures of them. The shops are very quaint, they all have open fronts and all customers go in and sit down and have a cup of coffee and a cigarette and then start to argue over the prices. This I am told takes hours sometimes, even over 1/- but as time is of no account here, it doesn't matter. The suburbs of the town are very quaint, being just mud hovels with camels, mules and fowls all living in the same room as the people. There is no drainage or attempt at sanitation so the effluvia is occasionally rather breezy. I was sent off this morning to a place on the Suez Canal and I am now in the train. On the right of us are miles and miles of desert, nothing but sand, and as one fellow remarked the only thing he regretted is that he didn't bring his bucket and spade. On our left is a belt of date palms, a few bananas and prickly pears, and then all sand again. The breeze is hot, just like from a furnace, but it is not an unpleasantly hot day and I am enjoying the trip.

The Egyptian is a very intelligent and shrewd man far better than the southern Europeans that I have met the last week or two. The Bedouin Arabs, of which there are a lot are very handsome pale and tall and I should think, fine fighters. The policemen are chiefly Nubians, and are real negroes, jet black and shiny with curly hair and lovely teeth, but poor features. They are dressed just as our police only with a fez instead of a helmet. The Sudanese are tall, thin and very intelligent, but the real good old fat Egyptian is the one I like. They ride about on their asses, or sit in the cafés round a hookah pipe and look just like the old boys in the *Arabian Nights*. I am quite sure this country hasn't progressed a bit since the Old Testament. The villages have their gates and walls, the sheik or headman living in what is considered here as a near approach to an English house, and there is always the mosque with its slender spire and the burial ground outside the walls. The whole place is like

Earls Court, but here it is the real thing and the sand and the flies make you realise it.

I could write about the East for hours, even after just being in it a day or two, but it must keep till later.

I wired home on my arrival and I hope you got it alright.
This letter is intended for you all as my time is very limited and I want this off at our next stop.

Now my own beloved, just a few words for you alone. This is a strange and wonderful land, full of new thoughts and ideas but not for one moment has your dear face been forgotten, nor have I done or thought of anything that you shouldn't know. It is a place full of temptations as you know, but you must trust me and whenever I return you will still find my lips and my heart have been quite pure for you. I want you to remember this because it may help you to bear the burden of our being separated. I am quite confident that you will be true to me and that is why I can enter into what I know is going to be a hard job quite calmly and cheerfully knowing that your thoughts and prayers are always with me.

You know I am no saint but now I am so far away I wish I had been better but I am quite convinced that my love is all for you and that it will never alter.

I can't say when I shall be able to write again but don't be despondent or unhappy. I shall be thinking of you always and whenever the mail does go there will be a letter for you if I can possibly manage it. As I am miles out in the desert you will understand the difficulties of writing and I believe the mail only leaves once a fortnight.

Help Mother as much as you can to be cheerful and I hope to be back soon.

Give my love to your Mother and Father, I am sorry I haven't been able to write yet but hope to do so soon.

With all my love. Your very own for ever, Norman.

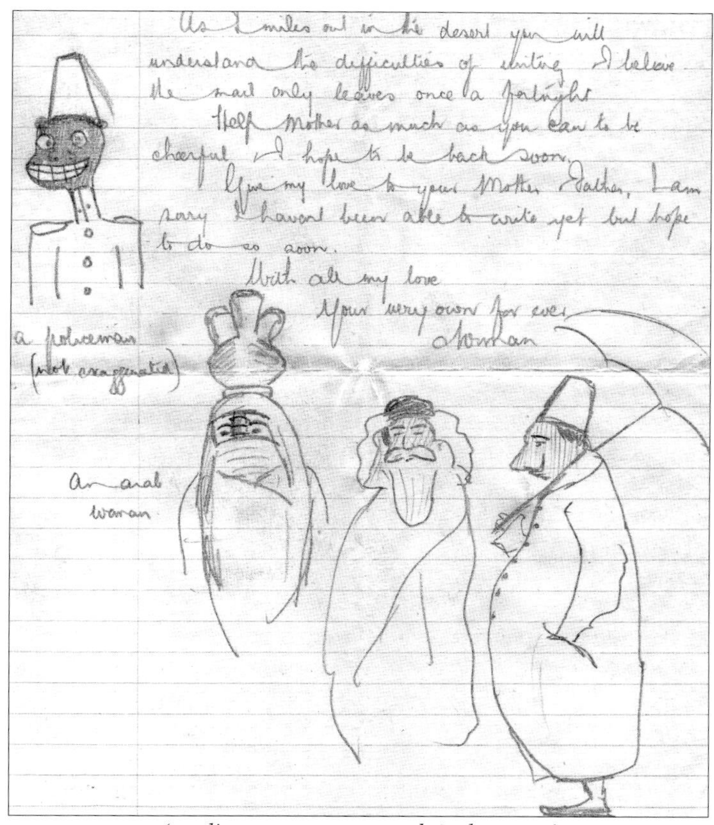

As [illegible] miles out in the desert you will understand the difficulties of writing I believe the mail only leaves once a fortnight

Help Mother as much as you can to be cheerful I hope to be back soon.

Give my love to your Mother & Father, I am sorry I haven't been able to write yet but hope to do so soon.

With all my love

Your very own for ever

Norman

'a policeman not exaggerated, Arab woman'
[*plus Bedouin and man in fez with umbrella*].

Extract from Amiel's Diary

[Subsequent entries only mention places where, I have assumed, Amiel and the Allies gave a show.]

Nov 3 Saturday	Vicarage Coleshill.
Nov 6 Tuesday	1 Camp Sutton [the first of two concerts here].
Nov 10 Saturday	Longfield 7pm.
Nov 13 Tuesday	Allies, Solihull.
Nov 17 Saturday	Hampton 7pm [Possibly this was Eastcote Hospital, Hampton in Arden.].
Nov 19 Monday	YMCA Worcester Street.
Nov 24 Saturday	Allies Churchfields.
Nov 28 Wednesday	Whitaker, Allies 7.30pm [Whitacre, Warwickshire].

Extracts from Norman's Diary

Nov 2 Friday	*Arrived Alexandria.*
Nov 3 Saturday	*Arrived Kantara.*
Nov 5 Monday	*Arrived Karim. My first real day at the front. Passed Gaza and saw the shells dropping there. Arrived at Karim, the detail camp for 53rd Division and there found Raymond and Bulmer. A Taube came over at 4.30 but was soon driven off. [Taube were German aircraft, originally used for combat but also used for observation.]*
Nov 6 Tuesday	*Marched from Karim to a spot on the Beersheba defences. Arrived there about 6 o'clock in the dark.*
Nov 7 Wednesday	*Left Beersheba for the Hereford Reserve Camp. Was attacked by 2 planes with machine guns but only 7 camels were hit.*
Nov 8 Thursday	*Went up to the front line. The camp is on a rocky hill on the summit of which are Bedouin caves. The battalion has lost heavily in the attack on the 6th. Lewis and Raylor both being wounded*
Nov 9 Friday	*Went out on a burial party over the battlefield but apparently was not affected by the sights.*

[Gaza blocked the way to Jerusalem. There were three battles of Gaza, the first being in March 1917. Poor leadership meant that the Turks were not overcome and a change of command came when General Allenby replaced Murray. Allenby's attack in October 1917 swept north and east. The third battle of Gaza when Gaza fell, also referred to as the Battle of Beersheba, took place during 27 October – 7 November. There were many Herefordshire casualties. Norman's diary entries for 5th to 9th November refers to this battle, and his letter of the 8th tells of having 'had a hard time of it lately but don't tell Mother'.]

Basecamp in the desert.

Basecamp in the desert.

1st Herefordshire Regt.
53rd Division
E.E.F.
Sunday 4th Nov 1917 [he's actually written 5th Nov]

My own beloved,

I am afraid there is very little of interest to tell you in this letter. I am still at the base in the desert but am probably moving higher up this afternoon. There is nothing but sand everywhere and I am sure in a month or two I shall long for the sight of a green field and some trees other then the eternal date palm. The East is a wonderful place – for a holiday – but I seem to miss you so very very much lately, and I cannot imagine how I am going to exist without you for perhaps a long while. We did have a good time in our sweetheart days, didn't we, and I am sure we shall have a better time in the days to come. Your love for me keeps me content but sometimes like just at this moment, I feel I want you so very much. It is Sunday morning, most glorious sunshine, and very hot, and reminds me of those many Sundays we have spent together in the summer. But I mustn't get depressed, I think my spirits are a bit low owing to a big thunderstorm in the night, you know how that always upsets me.

We had a concert party up here yesterday and they gave us a very decent show. It seemed so strange to hear all the old songs in this far off desert. We are in Asia now, not Egypt, but it is all the same, just sand everywhere. The Suez Canal is very interesting, it is so narrow and yet the biggest liners sail up it quite easily.

You wouldn't like some of the insects round here, moths are absolutely angels to them. I think the most horrible is what is called the flying beetle. It is shaped just like an ordinary black beetle, but is about the size of a small sparrow and it is most repulsive. The birds are very pretty, and there is any amount of hawks of a tremendous size.

It is troubling me to know what to do about a Xmas present for you. On no account must you send me one darling as it will probably never arrive or probably be damaged, and then we have to cut down the weight of everything so much. So if I am not home for Xmas, please keep whatever you thought of spending until I return. I shall be much more pleased if you will. As regards yours I am going to send you a wee cheque and I want you to just get what you like best. Please dearest don't be upset at my sending the money, but there are no shops here and you must have something from me. I shall enclose it in another letter and I hope it arrives in time.

There is very little more to say dearest, except that I love you and miss you more and more every day. Keep a cheerful heart and all will come right in the end, it is very hard to bear the separation I know, harder for you than for me because you are a woman, but all will come right. I can just hear the men singing the hymn *Jesu lover of my soul* and it does make me think of home. I wish they would dry up.

Well darling I must go now. Be brave, as I hope to be, and when weeks go without a letter, keep a cheery heart because things are very wild here and you can't expect modern postal arrangements 1000 miles from anywhere. I haven't had a letter yet from you, but I have my ring and my book and that is the sign of our great promise of love and I am satisfied.

I am very fit and well, don't think I am unhappy I am not, but just longing for a sight of you and a green field.

With all my love, Always your very (own) Norman
I enclose a bit of desert for you.

1st Herefordshires
53rd Division
Egypt
Thursday 8th Nov 1917

My own beloved,

I don't know when I can post this letter or when you can get it but I hope before Xmas. I am enclosing a cheque and want you to get something for my Mother with

£1, Father £1, and yourself £2. Now you mustn't be upset at my having to send a cheque, but I do want you to have something at Xmas.

We have had a very hard time lately but don't tell Mother about it, only I want you to know. We are marching day after day through the burning desert, very little food or water and occasionally under fire but nothing very serious. We had an aeroplane on us yesterday firing machine guns and that was most disconcerting. I don't feel I can write much now, and don't know when I shall be able to again as we are off once more still pushing forward. I love you even more, but in a much better way I am sure; you are to me out here my guiding angel and when I come home what happiness for us both it will be. I have just found a fellow on some camels who is going back to the base and he is taking this for me so goodbye for the present love, I will write as soon as I can. I am very fit and hope you are cheerful – be this for my sake and thank goodness you are at home and not here.

With all my love. Always your very own Norman.

[Norman refers to food and water shortages only briefly in his letter of 8th November but it was a serious problem. Another letter dated 15th December refers to a photograph of him washing in the desert, saying he only had a small amount of water in his mess tin to wash in. There were also munitions shortages, not only because of the difficulties of transport but because of strikes back home, which annoys Norman in his letter of 19th November.]

Norman with Lieutenant Bulmer.

Camping under shellfire.

Extracts from Norman's Diary

Nov 10 Saturday	*Nothing doing except an aeroplane dropping bombs. Left here for a spot on the Hebron Road about 4.30.*
Nov 11 Sunday	*Spent the day in resting in the new camp. Was very fed up and was glad to be with Bulmer, without him I should be very miserable. Played two games of chess with Chubb.*
Nov 12 Monday	*Rifle and kit inspection. Raymond, Trumper and Collins turned up I am glad to say but no letters yet.*
Nov 13 Tuesday	*Resting. No excitement and was rather fed up generally. Received a letter from Mother dated 25.10.17.*
Nov 14 Wednesday	*Resting.*
Nov 15 Thursday	*Nothing doing.*
Nov 16 Friday	*Very quiet day. Short route march in morning. Fried liver for breakfast as two sheep were bought from some Bedouins. Am tired of being here already and should like to be home again. Wrote to Amiel, also put in travelling claims.*
Nov 17 Saturday	*Went to wells near Beersheba for washing. These are 3000 years old and there were many Bedouins there.*
Nov 18 Sunday	*Went with 40 camels on salvage work. Had a letter from Amiel and Father.*
Nov 19 Monday	*Took party to the wells and got caught in a storm. Found my bivy deep in water and spent an unpleasant night.*

[Spending an 'unpleasant night' in a wet bivy bag is an understatement! The desert could be terribly hot, as described in his letters for 4th November and 2nd December. Others had said it was hot enough for the men to poach eggs in their tin hat. But during the evening of 19th November there had been a thunderstorm with a torrential downpour and in a few hours everywhere was in flood. The soil, hard in summer, became sticky and heavy going for soldiers and wheeled vehicles alike (see letter for 20th December). And night time temperatures plummeted. The men would have been marching in shorts and tunic in the hot desert and ill prepared for the change in weather with only a single blanket or great coat for protection. If they were lucky, or an officer, they might be given billets in houses, or a monastery (see letter for Christmas Day).]

19th November 1917

My very own darling,

I think I am about the happiest man in the whole regiment today and it is all because of your lovely letter last night. It was the first I have had and you have no idea how it cheered me up and if you knew how it was appreciated you would have to take a larger size in hats. I know just how much you feel you want me, I want you just as much and it does seem awful at times to have to exist without each other and I get so annoyed that I could kick anybody, but it really can't be helped dearest and we must be as patient as we can until we are reunited. I feel an awful way from you but your letter brought me very near to you and to home. As regards McGregor, will you please ask them to send you the passbook and not to transfer any more money to the National Provincial as I think they may be more considerate if I do this. They are a fearful nuisance but it can't be helped can it?

Dot seemed to have got quite a decent new job but I want you to stay at the Bank because it seems so nice to feel you are keeping my place for me. My address will always be the same '1st Herefordshire Regt, 53rd Division, E.E.F.' The great disadvantage of here is that there is no leave and also that even if I do get wounded or ill I cannot get home, it isn't a bit like France for that but we must put up with the inevitable and if the war is going to be over soon, all the better as everyone here has had enough. Please remember me to Jimmie and Mr Scarboro', it is kind of them to think of me.

I wish some of these munition people could come out here, a week here would cure all strikes and if you could see what the boys out here go through, you would never speak to a fit chap who is at home in munitions. [Munitions strikes in England meant serious shortages for the army.]

I wish I had some of your oatmeal cakes, and some marrow jam. I often think of it. [Amiel's mother's recipe for marrow jam is given towards the end of the book.]

There is a fellow who has come up here who is a master of Old Testament history, and I think I can tell you where we are by this. You remember when Moses sent spies out to find what the land was like, eight were unfaithful but two told of a land of milk and honey. To Caleb, one of these, he gave a town and this is where we are. We are in the land of the Amalekites and the Bedouins are Midianites. I had a most interesting experience yesterday, I took 20 men, 40 camels and a lot of natives up into the hills. We came to some wells [Beersheba Wells] which had been used by Moses and were over 5000 years old. The water was good but very milky and the original coping was there. A tribe of Bedouins came up to get water, they each carried two large amphorae which are sort of urns, and they are really wonderful people to watch. They are very tall and handsome, not very dark and very like pictures one sees of the 12 apostles. They were very friendly but of course they have to be, but I wouldn't trust them very far. We saw two jackals and had a shot at one, but he was too far off.

I came across a lot of white rats, and they were so tame they ate out of my hand. Things are very quiet here at present. I am afraid too good to last and I shall be oh so glad to hold you in my arms again. I enclose a bit of poetry I thought rather appropriate. [Sadly not found in the family archives.]

Night – I am writing this in my dugout by candlelight and just imagine you back from the Bank having your tea. How much I wish I could be with you darling, but I am patient and contented knowing it will all be there for me when I come home. I realise my many faults now I am out here but do hope you have forgiven me although I am sure of it as love forgives everything. It is pouring outside and this makes it seem more like England, and you, and I do so love you, every hour of the day I think of you. I sometimes wish we had married and yet we are just as much each other's and I am afraid I shall be in just a bit of a hurry when I do come home, but that is a long way off I am afraid. I will write again soon but until my next letter think of me each day and remember I am yours to the very end. Whatever I have been in the past is gone now I am sure, and my whole heart is just for my angel. Keep cheerful as that helps everyone so much as well as me. Give my love to your Mother and Father and a goodnight kiss for you.

With all my love. Your very own Norman.

Extracts from Norman's Diary

Nov 20 Tuesday	*Letter from Father.*
Nov 21 Wednesday	*Found a beetle which shams dead when touched.*
Nov 22 Thursday	*Felt fed up and tired – a sunny day but had to stay in camp. We often wonder how long we shall be out here even after such a short stay, we all feel we have had enough. The cold last night was very severe and no one had a good night. B & D Companies left for Beersheba to mend roads. Played snap with Chubb, Raymond and Linzell until 9.30pm.*
Nov 23 Friday	*Rode with the Padre to Beersheba to get stuff from the Canteen. Took photos of the Mosque Garden in the square, two of a Turkish house and garden and gathered some flowers to send to Amiel. Payed (sic) the Transport on the way back. All septic men put in an isolation camp.*
Nov 24 Saturday	*Went to Beer Hassan Wells for the day. Took two photos of Bedouins.*
Nov 25 Sunday	*Church Parade. Started from Tel el Sakarti at 1 o'clock and marched to Beersheba. Billeted in a decent house near Y.M.C.A. with Wilmot, Linzell, Collins. Heard hymns at Y.M.C.A. sung by Royal Welsh Fusiliers.*
Nov 26 Monday	
Nov 27 Tuesday	
Nov 28 Wednesday	*Went to Wadi Magir in lorries to mend roads and march back each evening. Had letter from Amiel. She feels doubtful and discontented.*

The Y. M. C. A.
With the Egyptian Expeditionary Forces
On Active Service
FIELD POST OFFICE
A
DE 10
17
Miss Amiel Robins,
191 Holly Road,
Handsworth
Birmingham,
England
PASSED BY CENSOR
No 3670

Envelope with Censor mark.

28th Nov 1917

My own dearest love,

I was ever so delighted to get your letter dated 25th Oct, although it was dated only 3 days after the former one it arrived 14 days later, so you can tell how the posts run here. It was I am sure the most beautiful letter you have ever written me, because although it was rather strange in places, yet you really showed me just how you felt and that is what I always want you to do. I can quite understand your feelings, haven't I often told you you are bound to get times of doubt and you must expect them and I am sure your love is strong enough to come out on top. I know just how lonely you feel without me and what a terrible feeling that is, but you must be brave and remember that my love for you is even greater now than it ever was. You are wrong when you say that this job is so big that it occupies my mind apart from you, that is not the case at all and if it wasn't for your dear face being always before me this place would be absolutely awful.

There is only one thing that keeps us going, it is the same for everyone out here, and that is hope, and my one hope is that when I come home I shall find my darling unchanged in love and ready to come to me. I certainly don't want you here with me, I often think that I have a great deal to be thankful for in knowing you are fairly safe. I couldn't rest a minute if you were here, because although I write home cheerfully and hopefully, sometimes the life out here gets awful and it is no place for a woman. I am not complaining in the least, it has got to be done and I am glad I can help the fellows to bring it off and we shall come out on top sooner or later, but all the same it is a hard task and no Cooks tour as some people imagine. I have your love and that is enough out here. Don't think I don't want you physically because I do, oh darling ever so much, and I daren't think about that side of it, but I must be patient and you must until we can have each other in peace and happiness. I don't know if you can understand what I mean. I feel so certain of you and your love that I could be happy and patient anywhere, just living in hope and the thoughts of the happy times to come.

Now let me tell you all the news. We are at present billeted!!! in a captured town and I am living in quite a decent house. It is quite empty of course and only a large sofa and a few odds and ends left in it but quite comfortable. It is quite large and would belong to probably a bank manager or someone of that class. There are only two rooms of course, as in all these houses, just a living room and a bedroom as the husband, wives and children all have the same room, visitors as well I expect unless they go on the roof which is flat. The house is surrounded by a huge thick wall about 30 feet high, no loopholes or windows in the wall, but one small door, these Turks must evidently like privacy. There is a large garden filled with acacia, orange, almond and fig trees and a couple of cypress. There is the usual well and a large portico.

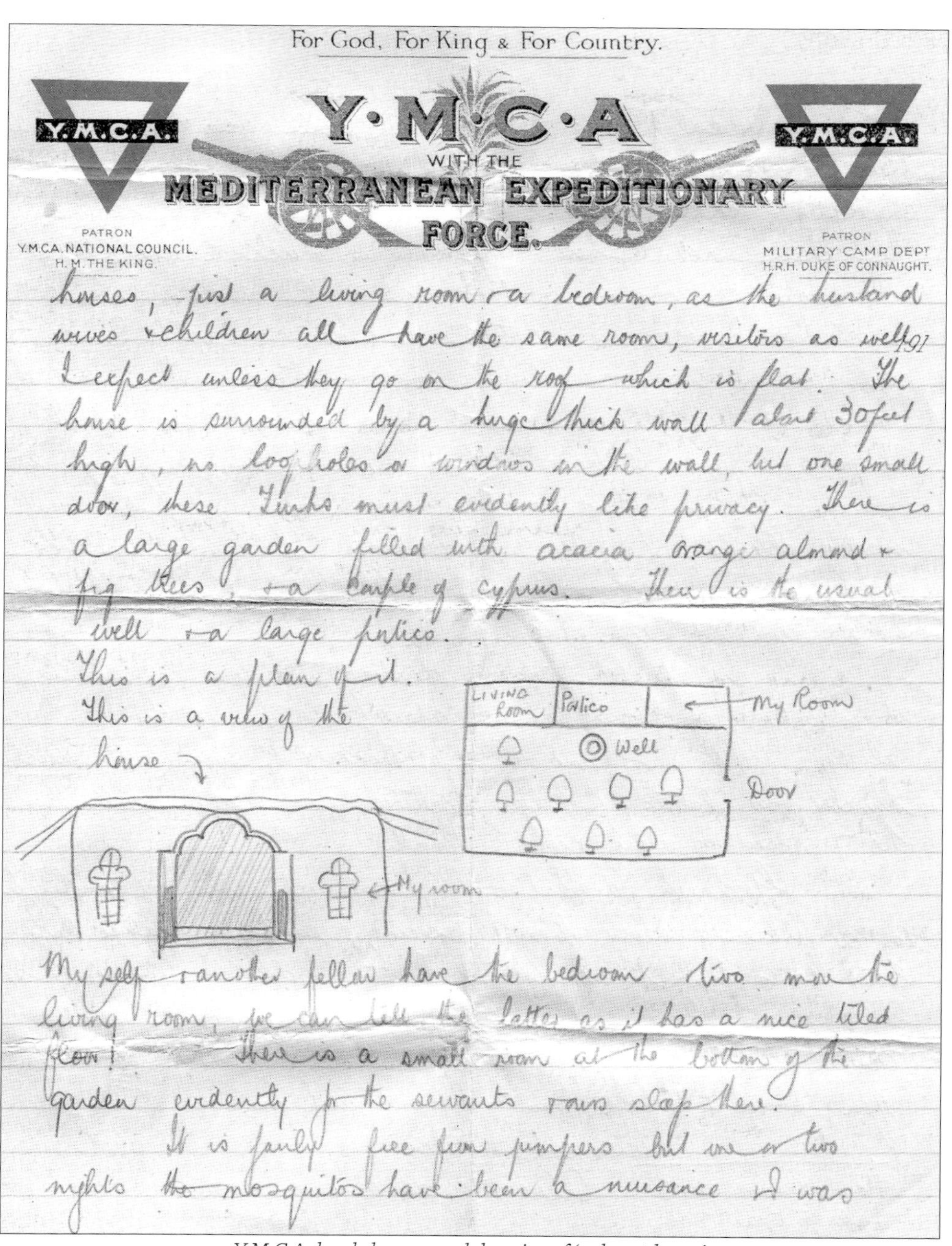

For God, For King & For Country.

Y·M·C·A

WITH THE MEDITERRANEAN EXPEDITIONARY FORCE.

PATRON
Y.M.C.A. NATIONAL COUNCIL.
H.M. THE KING.

PATRON
MILITARY CAMP DEPT
H.R.H. DUKE OF CONNAUGHT.

houses, just a living room & a bedroom, as the husband wives & children all have the same room, visitors as well I expect unless they go on the roof which is flat. The house is surrounded by a huge thick wall about 30 feet high, no loop holes or windows in the wall, but one small door, these Turks must evidently like privacy. There is a large garden filled with acacia orange almond & fig trees, & a couple of cyprus. There is the usual well & a large portico.

This is a plan of it.

This is a view of the house →

My self & another fellow have the bedroom two more the living room, we can tell the latter as it has a nice tiled floor! There is a small room at the bottom of the garden evidently for the servants to sleep there.

It is fairly free from jumpers but one or two nights the mosquitos have been a nuisance & I was

Y.M.C.A. headed paper and drawing of 'a decent house' referred to in letter above and below.

Myself and another fellow have the bedroom and two more in the living room, we can tell the latter as it has a nice tiled floor. There is a small room at the bottom of the garden evidently for the servants and ours sleep there.

It is fairly free from jumpers but one or two nights the mosquitoes have been a nuisance and I was bitten in several places but they are well again now. We have a decent mess here and best of all a Y.M.C.A. where chocolates and cakes (about as hard as the tiles) can be bought. We shall not be here long as it is much too comfortable, there are sparrows and swallows about and the mornings sound just like home again with the birds about. Last Sunday I felt rather like home and did so want you then. They had a service at the Y.M.C.A. and from our house we could hear all the hymns we get at home and home seemed then very near to us.

I am glad to say I am very fit and feel very merry and bright. We are working fairly hard making roads etc and I could stay here till the boat sails for home, but no such luck.

Try to be content darling with our separation, it is only our bodies that are apart, our hearts are always together and I am always thinking of you. We must number our letters, I keep forgetting so I will call this No. 7, that is about right I think.

Goodnight dearest one. I am writing this by candlelight in a place I never thought of seeing, can you realise this letter comes from the marvellous East; I do wish you could see it and see me here, I feel like Aladdin as I have a real Eastern lamp to light me up. Cheerio dearest, I do so love you and want to have you once more with me.

With all my love, Always your very very own Norman.
Please excuse mistakes but I am too tired to read this through.

Extract from Amiel's Diary

Dec 1 Saturday	Allies, St Gerards [Coleshill] 6.30pm.
Dec 5 Wednesday	Grand Hotel.
Dec 6 Thursday	2 Camp Sutton 7pm. [Second visit to Camp Sutton]
Dec 7 Friday	C. Pierrots 7.15pm. [Unable to decipher the first word]
Dec 8 Saturday	Longfield 7pm.
Dec 15 Saturday	Blackwell 5.30pm.
Dec 27 Thursday	Farcroft 6.30pm. [Auxiliary hospital in Handsworth]
Dec 29 Saturday	Stechford 6.30pm.
Dec 31 Monday	Longfield 6.30pm.

Extracts from Norman's Diary

Nov 29 Thursday	*Stayed in Beersheba and had a hot bath. 3 letters from Amiel. 2 letters from home. Wrote several Xmas letters.*
Nov 30 Friday	*Company Orderly Officer. Had a good hot shower bath in evening.*
Dec 1 Saturday	*Orderly Officer. Another letter from Amiel and three from home. An iguana has a home in a hut in our garden.*
Dec 2 Sunday	*Church Parade 8 o'clock. In afternoon went on a reconnaissance towards Auja and back to Hebron Road.*
Dec 3 Monday	*Went out on salvage work on Auja Road.*
Dec 4 Tuesday	*Salvage on Tel el Faba Road (Tel el Saba). Had letters from Amiel and Home.*
Dec 5 Wednesday	*Salvage in same place as yesterday.*
Dec 6 Thursday	*A piano arrived and we had some music after Mess by the Divisional concert party – much appreciated.*

[Y.M.C.A. paper]
Sunday 2nd Dec 1917

My own darling,

I had a great surprise yesterday by getting another letter from you dated 8/11/17, you are an angel to write such a lot and they are all such long ones too. I am afraid my letters seem very tame at the side of yours as you can put everything so well on paper. You seem to be doing very well at the Bank and I am so glad because I feel it is my work you are keeping on for me, I would much rather you were there than anywhere else. It is a pity my letters haven't been turning up well but you mustn't mind and must try to get reconciled to it. If you just think that at present I am 150 miles from a civilised town and miles away from a railway and everything has to go by camel you can understand that it is a wonder we ever get letters at all. I think the organisation of our Army is marvellous to be able to arrange such things because you must see that food and ammunition etc all has to come the same way, and to think they can find room for two such unimportant individuals as we are is very good of them.

As regards the Bank exam I think you are wise not to take it as it would be no use to you in the future. You see I agree with you that it is no use our waiting until all is straight again before we have our great happiness and as soon as we can you know I want us to get married and that will mean that you will have to give up the Bank. It is a good job you have so many shows on as they must take away your loneliness, at least for a time.

I had a rotten evening last night and I know I oughtn't to tell you but I feel I want to as I want you to know everything. I don't know what caused it or why I felt as I did, but it suddenly came into my mind what it would be like if I came back and found you didn't want me. I know it was very wrong of me to have felt as I did and now I feel awfully disloyal to you but I couldn't help it and I was so glad when this morning came to find all those silly feelings had gone and I was absolutely as positive of your love as I have ever been. It was a real evening of doubt and can you explain it – it was Saturday 1st December and happened about 5 till 7 in English time. I am quite all right again today but I feel very lonely and do wish I could see you just for a few minutes. I feel so far away and so helpless here and if it wasn't for your love to strengthen me when I am like this life would be awful.

Now I am getting very inched [sic] by upsetting you and myself so I must just buck up. I feel I should like to shake myself, but I can quite understand anyone being the same out here, I had noticed it in the other fellows. Usually they are all merry and bright and then suddenly a day will come and one of them will hardly speak and if I ask him what is the matter the answer is always the same from everyone of them 'It's all right old thing, I am having an off day and am simply fed up to the teeth'. If you knew the awful stillness of the East, not a breath of wind, the almost brazen glare of the sun on the yellow mud caked houses, the absence of everything but khaki, you perhaps would understand. This part must be wonderful for a holiday but to live here, particularly now, is worse I think than a short and merry life in the line.

I understand we are likely to remain here some time and I must be thankful, as we are quite safe here and our line has advanced so far that we are out of all danger. It is Sunday today and that is always very dull with us. I have managed to fix up a football match for this afternoon, but what we need most of all is a piano. We have a harmonium from a Turkish mission but that doesn't act very well and the men want waking up, we all do, I feel we are getting like the tortoises and you can't tell how the feeling riles one. To want to be up and doing and yet have nothing to do is even worse than hardships sometimes.

You will think this a very strange letter but it is such a great relief to have you to whom I can just put all that is inside me and I know you will understand. I daren't write all this and send it home and perhaps I am wrong in burdening you with all my fancies, but I feel that now you have accepted my love you are willing to take on the more painful things as well and I suppose that is what a lover and a wife is for. You know I always want to know everything about you – just everything.

I had a magazine the other day and there was a tale called 'Letters she never sent' and although it was very poor stuff yet there was a lot of truth in it and I felt had she only sent those letters, which really contained her heart, to her fellow, he would have understood her and loved her all the more.

I know I am not a bit good and I am sure during life I shall do heaps of mean and rotten things and if I do I want to feel I can tell them all to you and still know I have your love, and I want you to be just the same with me. I have no secrets from you up to now and I hope I never shall.

I hear Bernard is likely to join the Indian Army, it may suit him but not me, all I want is you and I can only get you by the war ending.

It is remarkable how everyone seems to think it will end soon, I am most optimistic myself, why I can't tell and when it does darling, what a time we will have.

I am sure I don't know what I shall do when I know I am coming home to have you just for myself. I often try to imagine our feelings when we (you and I) get in the train for that first fortnight, all on our own and nothing to think of but love. I mustn't let my feelings carry me too far as it is no use, but still the fact remains that that time is coming and every day means a day nearer, every letter I send one less before I can call you something more than sweetheart.

Please forgive me writing all I have, I shall not read this through as I may have said too much and feel I oughtn't to send this letter but I feel heaps better by getting it all off my chest. I am fit and as happy as I can be without you and home. Look at our picture often and remember you are always in my thoughts.

With all my love, Always your very own Norman.
I do love you angel.

[Y.M.C.A. paper]
4th Dec 1917

My own beloved,

I am afraid my last letter to you was not a very cheerful one and I hope you have forgiven me for sending it, as I really oughtn't to write anything which will worry you as I know you are having quite enough to bear at the present time. I am very merry again now but would like to get hold of a piano.

The flies today are a fearful nuisance, I can't think how they have all got into the house, as we have been so free from them up to now. At night we have many visitors and the advertisement that my sleeping bag was vermin proof is hardly strictly truthful. At least there is something each night which bites and keeps me awake, and I have bathed enough to drown it by now. Did you get the card I sent you, it was not very elegant but I got one or two like it from a fellow who had been to Alex. I have sent my films to Cairo with a fellow who has a week's leave, and I hope in a week or so to be able to send you some results if they are any good and don't get pinched in the post. The enclosures in this letter are a sheet out of the Koran and an army form I found in a Turkish trench. The alphabet consists of 29 letters I am told and the people read from right to left and start at the end of the book. Talking about books I heard a good problem the other day and no catch in it. A man has a 3-volume novel, each volume containing 100 pages. The thickness of the cover of each book is 1/2 inch and the thickness of each book without covers is 1 inch.

These books are put in order 1, 2 and 3 vol, in a bookcase. A worm enters between the cover and page 1 of Vol.1 and eats through to page 100 Vol.3, what distance has he covered? It is not 5 inches as you may imagine and I will tell you the answer in my next letter if I remember. [See 10th December.]

As regards my doings lately things have been fairly interesting. On Sunday I took a horse and went for a long ride over some old battlefields to look for salvage such as rifles, equipment, ammunition etc. On Monday and Tuesday and again today we have been collecting the stuff and bringing it in. The Turks must have left this part in a fearful hurry as everything has been left and some of the things we found were very strange. We found a Singer sewing machine, a chip potato carl [sic] and an English cookery book, several German books and a copy of the Koran, and of course heaps and heaps of military things such as live shells, bombs etc.

I had my first Jaffa oranges yesterday. I met an Arab who had a sackful and I bought a dozen off him although this is strictly against all rules but I couldn't resist them. I may say we soon finished them off, I had the last one just before starting this letter. I understand there is going to be a separation allowance for officers – another reason why we might have – but never mind you are mine just as much although I daresay an extra pound a week would come in useful for you.

There is very little fruit about here now, we never even get dates, why I can't tell. I saw my first eagle this morning and would have liked a shot at him as he was huge but we are not allowed to shoot at animals or birds. I think the reason for all these restrictions is to impress on the natives that we are really a decent nation and not the folks the Germans have made out. I couldn't think why this eagle was following me, at first I thought he meant to have a go for me or the horse, but that would have been very unlikely as they get heaps of food about here in the shape of dead horses and camels, although he was quite big enough to go for a human being. He must have been 8 or 10 feet between the tips of his wings and was horrible in the face. I found the reason for his visit after going a few yards as I found a poor Turk who had stopped a bullet. He had been dead some weeks and we soon buried him and when it's all said and done I suppose he has relations at home and probably someone waiting for him like I have. By this time I ought to be used to such sights for goodness knows I have seen enough to last a lifetime although I have purposely kept off such topics when writing to you and home, but every time I see a chap laid out whether he is brown or white I can't help thinking what a fearful madness this war is. I have never forgotten standing one day some weeks ago with a Scotchman, quite an old chap, and we saw a lot of boys going up into the line just before the push, and he said to me "You can't beat that sort, but laddie they're just too good to be killed", and I always think of what he says when I see such things as this morning.

But you will think I am getting an old misery and I am not a bit, I am feeling as merry and well as I ever did, but dearest it is such a relief to have someone like you to write to so that I can put down everything. I can tell you better what I mean when I get back and I do hope that will be soon as I am longing to see you again.

I have suddenly heard that there is a mail in and on dashing up to the mess I was delighted to have a lovely long letter from you and also one from home. Apparently you haven't received any letters from me for some time but by now they are certain to have turned up again. If you only knew how much I loved your letters you would have to have a very extra large size in hats. I am glad you got a rise of 2/6, I am sure you deserve it and it all helps doesn't it? I can quite understand you are glad we didn't marry, I am afraid I am selfish when I keep saying I wish we had, but you must be patient with me, it is only the knowledge that your love will last for ever that makes me contented here. I must finish off this letter now as I want it to go today if possible.

I do love you, and want you every minute of the day and honestly my first thought in a morning and last at night is about you and always will be. I do hope we are happy when we get married but I have <u>no</u> doubt about that at all and let us hope we can bring it off soon now. If the people who were keeping this war going could only see the side of it that we get here and in France, they would never sleep again. We have got to see it through but I trust the end is getting near as I do want you with me again. I suppose we both have two natures, physical and mental and both mine need you very very much – oh darling when you are really mine for ever what peace it will be for us.

With all my love, Always your very own Norman.
This is a long letter but I am afraid rather dull, never mind better to have a quiet life out here than one too lively – and it can be that when the Turks stop running for a bit.

Thursday 6th Dec 1917

My own beloved,

You will be surprised to know that this letter is being written with the luxury of a chair and a table, for the first time since I came out here and it is a great treat, perhaps soon I shall sport a pen and ink, you never know. We are very happy and comfortable still in the old Turkish town, I expect you have guessed where it is by this time, and I only hope we can spend Xmas here. I feel quite at home here now and shall really be sorry to leave it unless of course I am leaving it to come to you, which is hardly on the cards just yet. My servant was taken fearfully ill the other night, he is a very nice boy and comes from Ross, and he is really very bad. I was awakened by his moans and went out to him, he lives in the room at the bottom of the garden with the other servants and I think he has a dose of rapid dysentery and that is the worst kind. He has gone to hospital now but I shall be glad to see him back again. One of the fellows billeted with me went off to hospital, he was very done up as he has been here now 3 years and in that time one's blood gets very thin in such a hot climate and I think he is sure to get home – I hope he does although we all want to be there soon.

Dear old Mogridge is out with me of course, he isn't in my billet as he is in another company – mine is A – but I see a lot of him. This life seems to alter them all, they all get so old and staid, all except me, and really I often wonder why it is. I see fellows of 19 and 20 who talk and act as though they were 80 and I can't feel a bit old myself, I suppose it must be my love for you that does it, they aren't all as lucky as I am.

A piano has arrived I don't know whose it is or how long it will stay, but I saw it on a Transport Waggon in the High Street today and I understand there is to be a grand concert tomorrow night. I wonder what these Arabs will think of the English music, they never seem to sing or smile, but perhaps they have cause to be sad, seeing their land overrun by a lot of heathens as they think us. The Gippos, that is the men from down the Nile way, are very different, they sing all day long a sort of Gregorian chant. I wonder if music in its infancy is always in the minor and consisting of about five notes because our own music was. This certainly is. The music itself I am told is their tribal music and the words are about their daily labours etc. A soloist sings a verse, or rather chants it, and the rest come in with a chorus, and those goes on for hours. One very popular air which one part are always singing is as follows:-

I don't know what the words mean, no-one seems to know, but you can get an idea of the tune I think. It is a melancholy sound when heard for more than half an hour and you feel as if you want to throw something at them.

Have you ever read any of Mrs Humphry Ward's books, I have just finished my first today *Helbeck of Bannisdale*. I am afraid I should have given it up long ago but I had nothing else to read so I just had to go on, but it is not to be recommended, it is all in religion and ends up rottenly, although I must admit it is a clever book. We have had no papers or magazines for over a month now so we are just about used up. I read a 'Union Jack Library' the other day all about Sexton Blake the detective and thoroughly enjoyed it, so that shows my brain must be going backwards instead of forwards.

We had a big dose of fleas last night, they must be fleas because they bite, although I can't find them. Anyway we got a sprayer today and all my clothes, sleeping bag etc have been thoroughly gone through so the flea colony must be sad tonight as my bed will be a most unhealthy spot for them to rest and feed. People in England make a fuss over one harmless little one, but they ought to be here, fleas go about in tribes. Never mind, we are still smiling.

Talking of tribes, the dogs here are very dangerous and I believe carnivorous. They roam about in large packs and at night it is rather unpleasant to meet them. The jackals too are not nice but they don't come near a town so we haven't seen any lately.

I hope this letter isn't boring you – it seems all about nothing in particular, but I like to write and tell you just everything I am doing and thinking of.

Friday
We had a topping evening yesterday, the piano I spoke of turned up at our mess and after dinner the Divisional concert party came in to give us a concert. They really are fine and I did enjoy hearing some music again, but one fellow sang ever so many of your songs *Until; Love Lyrics* etc and they made me feel just a bit homesick. We are having a concert for the men tonight. Wouldn't you like to spend this afternoon with me, I have the house to myself, everyone else is out and I have a dozen oranges – it would be lovely. I want this letter to go today so I must finish off. I do so love you darling, more and more every day and all I think of is when we shall meet again. Don't have any fears about my love changing, I am absolutely certain of that, and may we come together soon, I am always longing for that day when you will come to me for ever.

With all my love,
Always your very own, Norman.

[Incidentally, the author Mrs Humphry Ward translated the Journal by Henri Frédéric Amiel from French into English, published in 1885, which was so admired by Lewis Robins that he named his only child after him.]

[On Y.M.C.A. paper]
Saturday 8th Dec 1917

My very own Love,

We have been having some very heavy rain the last day or two and we are all so glad we are in decent dry houses. As I told you in my last letter, there was a concert for us last night but we had to postpone owing to the wet. I expect you have a show on tonight and don't I wish I could be there to see and enjoy it, also bring you home. I think we would sport a taxi all to ourselves if I could, but I mustn't think of such things or I shall be getting miserable.

While I think about it – you will be getting to know my balance at McGregor's every so often and should it ever accrue about £20 would you please transfer the excess to the N.P.? I am not expecting this to happen often but if it does, draw a cheque on McGregor's and post it to Hereford as they will never transfer it without. I expect you will think me awfully strange over my two huge accounts but until I got here and was settled I was really unable to tell quite how money was needed here. I find my expenses are not over much although of course food is frightfully dear in the mess owing to transport difficulties. If I keep a balance of about £20 at McGregor's it will see me through. I hear some rumour that our pay has been increased 2/- a day but don't know if it is right. My pay is roughly 7/6 (+ rumoured 2/-) and about 3/6 allowances per day so you will be able to tell from my pass book if I am getting it alright. I am giving you a lot of trouble but I am quite certain you don't mind because as you know it is your money as much as mine.

I do wish I could have seen *Daddy Long Legs* with you – never mind, home soon I hope now.

Now there's another matter. Your *Bystander* subscription finishes about Jan 15, so dearest will you please renew it for another 6 months and draw a cheque for the amount on McGregor's? [This was a weekly tabloid magazine, popular during WW1 for its trench humour cartoons.] I ask you to do this as a great favour and pleasure to me, and I hope you will see it in that light. Whatever you do don't pay for it with your own money or give up having it – please. It seems strange I know to ask you to do this for me instead of my sending a cheque from here – but think; I haven't any cheques, I don't know the amount, and I don't know the name of the bookseller; so please as a kindness to me do as I tell you and let me know by return that you have done it.

This is quite a business letter isn't it but try not to be bored, as a matter of fact I am sure you are not.

Sunday 9th Dec 1917
Sunday today and I haven't been to church. We have to carry on here just the same as any other day but I don't mind a bit as I hate having nothing to do. I have just been lying down reading and my right hand has got the cramp so I can hardly write this letter. We had a fine concert last night, it really was an excellent show and all the time I was thinking of you doing your show at another concert. It was held in a large barn, there was a good stage fitted up and electric light from a dynamo on a lorry. It all seemed to take us back home again, the party wore orange and black costumes and the stage was well draped in the same colours. One fellow, as the girl member of the troupe was great, and his costume splendid. It was given him by the General. They sang heaps of new songs and all the jokes were new – one good song was *I want to be Somebody's Baby* and another *Down where the Swanee River Flows.* There was a fellow who sang the *Love Lyrics* very well and a good cellist. They are giving another concert tonight to the coloured troops who are with us and I have been invited and shall be there – I do wish I could take you along with me. I wonder if you would be nervous with about 500 handsome niggers giving you the glad?

Do you think my letters are lacking in sentiment and that I am getting cold? I often feel l don't send you the sort of letters you want and yet darling I love you heaps more than I ever did – the right kind of love too I am sure.

I really won't let myself think too much about our future happiness, when I do I get so fed [up] with the present, that life gets unbearable almost. Sometimes the end of this war and our happiness to come, seems very near and then again it seems just as far away. If you will only trust me as I am sure you do you will find times go much happier. There are no temptations here of course, but I know quite well what the East is and any stories you get in England never give you a tenth of the real evils that go on out here. You must therefore trust me thoroughly – I have promised to come back to you as I left you and I shall. Your lips were the last that touched mine and they will be the very first in the future too, so just remember that always. When my letters seem cool, I hope they never do they are not meant to be, just remember I am keeping all my love for you deep down in my heart, and it will be there always.

I must go now darling. I hope you are very well and cheerful and also your Mother and Father, I will write them again as soon as I get any more news.

Keep brave, you have a harder task than I, but we shall both come through all right never fear.
With all my love. Yours for ever, Norman.

[On Y.M.C.A. paper]
Monday 10th Dec 1917

My own beloved,

I find the best way of writing to you is to jot down a few lines each day when I get a few minutes to myself. Have you noticed how this works in my letters, you have been keeping them I expect and when I come home they will give us a complete diary of the war out here as far as I am concerned. I heard that someone has to go to Cairo for a week or two so naturally I wanted to go, but I am very much afraid there is not the least chance of my going, in fact it is almost impossible, but all the same it would have been nice. There are so many places of interest out here that I feel I want to see them all before I return and yet I am dying to get back to you. I know I shall be disappointed if I come home without seeing Cairo and Luzor [Luxor] etc and yet I would come back to you tomorrow if I had the chance and all these places could go to blazes.

I went to the concert last night – Sunday – and did enjoy it, and the niggers did too. They are real American niggers from Jamaica, as black as ink and all smiles and of course they understand English – it is the only language they know.

There were plenty of ragtimes, including our old friend *Yaka Hoolah* – do you remember the last time we heard that sung – I thought about it last night. [This was a fake Hawaiian tune, the most popular song of summer in 1916. See note following N's letter of 18th Feb.]

It is about time another mail come in, it is a week since I heard from you so I am hoping to get a letter in a day or two now.

Tuesday
Last night I had great joy as there was a letter from you, an old one from Marseilles and one from your Mother. I am so sorry to hear that up to the time of writing you have had no letters, but I expect they are there alright now or I would wire you, as I am sure you must be just a little bit worried although you say you are not. So my little cherub is still just a little frightened of me, you really mustn't be dearest. I quite understand, or at least I think I do, that for any girl with any decent feelings at all the idea of getting married must be rather terrifying. All the same it has to be done when people are as much in love as we are – it is the only choice we have, so you must trust me and I will really do my utmost to help you to be really happy from the very start. We mustn't build too much on an early marriage because you can't tell a bit how this war will go on but we must hope for the best. When the time does come you will find me not a bit as awful as you must imagine – you make me feel like an old Blue Beard or something the way you talk – but I do know just what you mean and remember love gets over all that. Thousands of girls have had the same fears and they have managed all right in the end.

I think it is a great pity Dot can't be happy about Aubrey – if I had doubts as he must have I should go dotty being so far away from you and not being able to talk things over – letters are so unsatisfactory aren't they – there is no satisfaction in them like one short hour with you darling could give us both.

It is nearly a year now since I first saw you and honestly dearest this last has been my very happiest year even though I have had a few hardships. These are nothing, though, when I know there is a real love at home waiting for me. You are not a girl now, as you were when I first met you – I can tell the change even more than you perhaps and you have no idea how much better and more lovable you seem now. I don't want you to get old a bit but I have wanted you to get as you are now and that is a real loving grown woman whom I can feel will be a great help to me always through life – whatever troubles or joys we may meet. Your letters always make me feel stronger and better able to wait any length of time for the end. I do love you darling – do you think my love is the right sort yet – I hope so but I think you do.

With all my love, Always your very own Norman xxx
I will answer your Mother's letter in a day or so.
I hope there are not many mistakes in my letters I never read them through, it seems to spoil the idea of their being just talks to you.

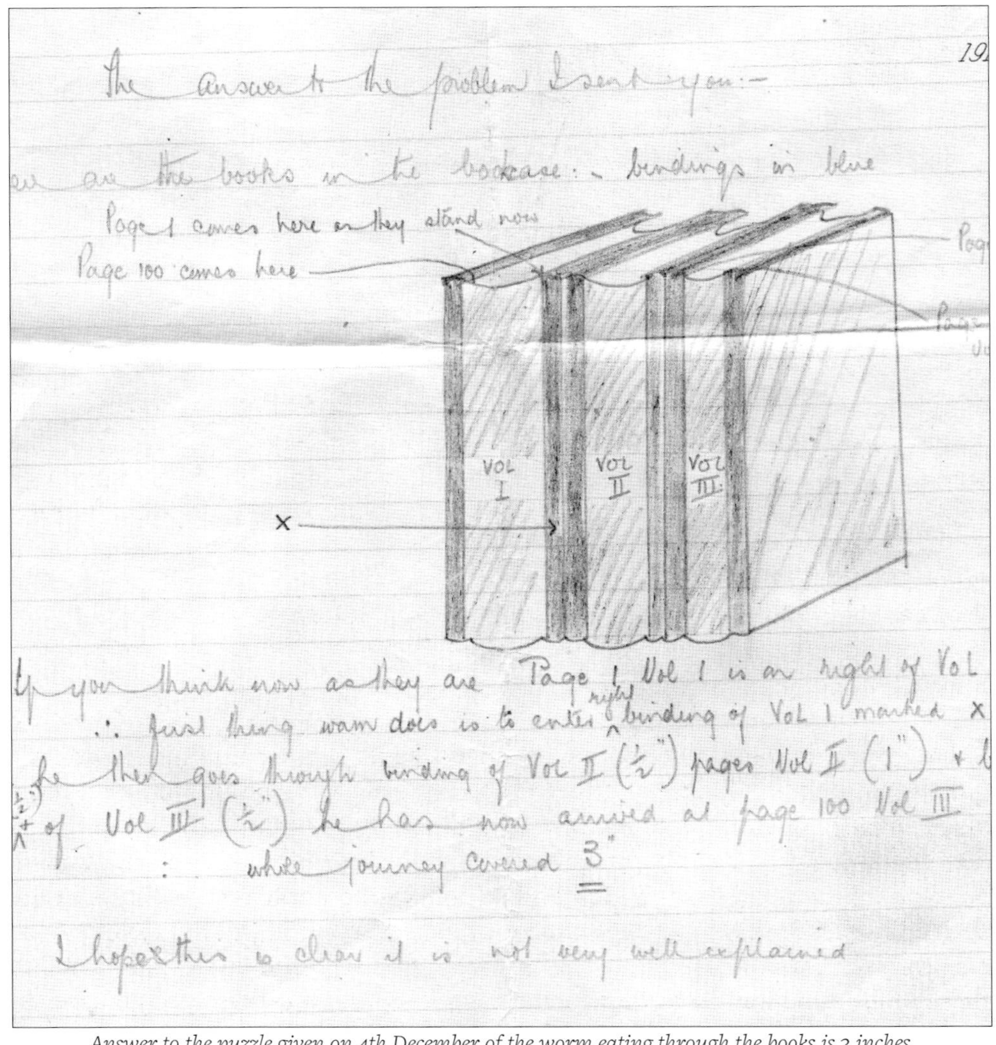

The answer to the problem I sent you:–

are the books in the bookcase:– bindings in blue

Page 1 comes here as they stand now
Page 100 comes here

VOL I
VOL II
VOL III
X

If you think now as they are Page 1 Vol I is on right of Vol I
∴ first thing worm does is to enter right binding of Vol I marked X
he then goes through binding of Vol II (½") pages Vol II (1") + ½" of Vol III (½") he has now arrived at page 100 Vol III
∴ whole journey covered 3"

I hope this is clear it is not very well explained

Answer to the puzzle given on 4th December of the worm eating through the books is 3 inches.

Extracts from Norman's Diary

Dec 7 Friday	*Went for route march along Auja Road and did drill coming back. There was to have been a concert but too wet. Two papers and a letter from home.*
Dec 8 Saturday	*Usual training during day. Had a concert by the Welsh Rabbits in a shed near the station – very good.*
Dec 9 Sunday	*Went to mend a road over a wadi on the Hebron Road near Sakarty. Another concert in the evening for the B.W.I. but was invited and very much enjoyed. Had dinner on return. Had to light a fire it was so cold. Fall of Jerusalem.*
Dec 10 Monday	*Stayed in all day.*
Dec 11 Tuesday	*Training in morning. Digging party near Sakarty in afternoon with Wilmot and Rooks. Played cards with Rooks and Moody.*
Dec 12 Wednesday	*Training in morning. Digging at No.2 Bridge in afternoon.*
Dec 13 Thursday	*Have a bad head and swollen glands probably due to smoke from our fire. Digging on road all morning.*
Dec 14 Friday	*Stayed in all day.*
Dec 15 Saturday	*Found a donkey in a terrible condition and had it shot.*

[Allenby captured Jerusalem as 'a Christmas present for the British people' so said David Lloyd George. The Turks surrendered on 9th December and on the 11th, General Allenby entered Jerusalem on foot in deference to the Holy City. During November and December Allenby had made enormous territorial gains, unlike on the Western Front, but it was at the expense of about 18,000 men, some casualties, some dead.]

[On Y.M.C.A. paper]
Saturday 15th Dec 1917

My own dear Love,

There has been very little happening since I last wrote to you, we just jog along very quietly here eating and sleeping. My servant made me a fine bed yesterday, it has a wooden framework and is covered with wire netting and you would be surprised how awfully comfortable it is, much better than the boards I have been sleeping on up to now. This morning I found a poor old donkey and I have never in my life seen such a terrible sight. He was like a skeleton and his backbone was right through his skin with sores. He had been left in some stable ages ago I should think, by some of these Arabs as he was no further good for work – it is a way these people have. As soon as I heard about him I went and had a look at him and as he was beyond any hope I got permission to have him shot. This was a fearful job as everyone is so afraid of offending the natives but I got it after an hour's running about and we finished off the poor chap. I only wish we could get hold of the men who left him, they would be sorry they were alive – they would get 50 lashes and although perhaps you can't believe it of me, I should like to give it them myself. If you had seen such a sight it would have made you weep, it nearly made me and I am afraid I am getting very hardened to the evils of the world now. You will have a bit of a job to soften me down again although I don't know, I think the more one sees of wrongdoing, the more one appreciates right. You know what Kipling says 'trust no man east of Suez' and I think he is about right, the things that go on in the East you would never believe possible, if I told you them, and I am sure I shall not do that, at least someday perhaps I might.

Oh I do wish you could be here dearest, my servant has just brought in a big bag full of the most beautiful Jaffas, huge ones and all ripe. I am just going to tackle one now so cheerioh.

Norman in Italy.

Norman in front of ridge tents in desert.

Norman and others, including Mogridge. Note bottle of wine!

Norman washing in the desert.

I am enclosing 4 snaps of myself, I hope those I sent in my last letter arrived safely. All the fellows here say the one taken in Italy looks like the Prince of Wales in the cinema, but I trust not. The one where I am washing misses the best bit of the photo, as I was having to use a mess tin, it is all the water we could get then, but it comes out in the film alright. It is not mud I am kneeling on but very fine sand. I think they have all come out splendidly thanks to your present, [Amiel gave him the camera] you have no idea how I appreciate it and it is nice to know that I had it from my Topsy, it is much better than if I had bought it myself, and you had given me something else. Please explain to Mother that I will send them copies of the same photos as soon as I can get some more printed, but I have had only one print of each at present, and I don't know when anyone else will be going down to Egypt again.

I always feel my letters are very cool nowadays, but they really are not meant to be, I love you honestly more and more every day and feel the need of your love more than ever. If you could only know what a great help you are to me out here you would be quite happy and contented. Your share of the war may not be very obvious, except as regards the Bank, to other people, but you are doing really more than anyone can tell to keep one fellow fit and happy and able to do his job, and that is more than most people can say.

I have found that the knowledge of your love is an absolute necessity to me while I am here and you will realise it when I come back even if you don't do so now. I am hoping to get a letter in a day or two now, the post is the one thing in life. Always remember dearest that I am yours and just as loving as I used to be even if I don't always seem to appear so in my letters.

I went in a house yesterday and found a slab in the floor with an inscription in Greek, and evidently a Christian as there was a cross on the stone. I am very anxious to find out what it is as such things are rather rare in a Moslem town. I must leave this for the present so cheerio dearest, I will continue later.

Sunday 16 Dec
I am going to finish off this letter today as I think there will be a mail going out. I thought I might have had a letter last night but I didn't – the posts just come any how, sometimes one a day for three days then none for a fortnight, I expect they only can send up letters when there is room in the transport.

Well darling I'll close now. I do wish I was with you this lovely Sunday morning, but it can't be so I am quite patient knowing you are mine for ever. I hope your show was a success last night, I thought of you many times.

With all the love I have, Always your own Norman.
Just take care of yourself this winter and keep free from colds.

Extracts from Norman's Diary

Dec 16 Sunday	*Suddenly moved from Beersheba at 4 o'clock to a well 4 miles north of Sakarty. [Tel el-Sakarti] Had to wait until 10 for our valises and supper.*
Dec 17 Monday	*Not very pleased with the place we are in – am going on picquet with my platoon tonight. [which means keeping watch]*
Dec 18 Tuesday	*Started to march at 11am. Passed through Dhiorich and some most wonderful scenery. Had trying experiences in the dark and rain and arrived at Alaka at 8pm.*
Dec 19 Wednesday	*Rained hard all night. Started to march again at 9.30 and had a pleasant time arriving Hebron 2 o'clock. Here we relieved D Company and were billeted in a large house. Visited the commissioner and the Turkish Doctor.*

Palestine
Monday 17th Dec 1917 [postmarked 22 Dec 1917]

My own dear Love,

You will probably be surprised to hear that we are once more on the move. We were very annoyed when we were told we had to leave those nice houses, but never mind I am still smiling and hope the war will end soon. We did a long march yesterday but it didn't tire me overmuch. My company has been left here and the others have gone on ahead, why I don't know. We are out on the desert again and it isn't too pleasant with dust and sand after such a topping 3 weeks as we have just had. Of course it has hardly been like active service and we knew it couldn't last for ever, but it is a pity we couldn't stay over Xmas, we could have had such a good time. I managed to get off a letter to you just before we left – and I shall not be able to get this off for some days probably now we have started to trek. We are going up into the most interesting part of this country, so for that part of it am rather pleased we are going.

We get heaps of rumours about the war in general, but in any case I feel that the end can't be very far off, I hope for both our sakes it isn't, as I do so want to see you again, so much so that I hardly dare think about it at times, I don't know why, but Sunday is always the worst day and I am absolutely dreading Xmas without you. Never mind dearest, it isn't going to last for ever and we shall appreciate it all the more when our time does come. Pray hard for peace as I am sure you do and it will come all in good time.

Thursday [20th Dec]
We have had a most exciting time since I wrote you the above. I and my platoon were left after the company had gone on and we had a night all on our own – just 25 of us – miles from anywhere. We started off next day and had a very long march through terrible rainstorms. We came through mountain gorges and torrents, heavy mists and then bleak stretches over the tops of the hills. We saw some of the most wonderful scenery I have ever seen – you can't imagine it at all. Have you ever been up Snowdon, it was just like that, all precipices and passes with huge rocks hanging over you. We passed through a large native town, one of the most peculiar places you could ever see. Probably until the war these people had hardly seen a white man as this is well off the caravan route, and we quite enjoyed the experiences while it was light. When the darkness came it was rather bogie, walking along narrow roads on the edge of the valleys and hardly being able to see 100 yards ahead. All this while we had heavy icy rainstorms and heaps of lightning and I was very glad when we were getting near our fellows again. On one hill our one and only wagon stuck and we were delayed about an hour trying to shift it. We couldn't leave it because it had our food etc onboard and I thought at one time we should never shift it but at last we did and then just over the hill we saw the lights of the remainder of our company. We camped there for the night with lovely rain coming down all the time. Luckily I was not very wet next morning but some of the fellows were and several were rather done up after the march.

We started again yesterday and had another long march – still in the mountains and valleys and then suddenly we turned over a hill and saw a most wonderful sight – no wonder Abraham called it a land of milk and honey – we saw a high valley full of gardens with almonds, mangoes, pomegranates, figs etc, beautiful tilled land with vegetables, plenty of good grass – the first I have seen here – and at the back of it all the most wonderful town you can think of. The fellows were absolutely bucked at this and they all pushed on splendidly. We passed a large white stone monastery and into the town passed fine houses all covered with vines and creepers, heaps of civilians and white people in European clothes and best of all people speaking English again and the women dressed as we are used to seeing them. We passed a large hotel, up the main street with shops in full swing. Here we were met by the Brigadier and the C.O. of the Herefords and we were told that after all our trying times our company was to be the garrison of this town.

I wish I could tell you where we are but I can't. We are now in the heart of the biblical world – Abraham is buried here and his tomb is in the mosque [Hebron] – and all around are many interesting sights. I am living in a large country house with a big garden and orchard and am having each day full of adventures. The people are most kind and friendly – the late Governor is quite a decent young fellow – a Turk of course – and the head of the hospital is one of the best, I spent a good time with him last night. All the inhabitants seem very glad to have us here and the baker calls for breakfast with hot rolls for us and an old French woman brings eggs. How long we shall be here I can't say – it seems too good to last for very long. Unfortunately the weather is bad and I have not been able to get any photos of this place as yet but I hope to do so. There is no danger here at all so don't think there is.

Will you please read the interesting parts of this letter to Mother as I have an awful lot to do – there are only 5 officers to run this town including the governor – so you can tell I don't get much spare time, but we are dry and happy and well fed and what more can anyone want? But I do want one thing and that is you dearest and soon I hope to come back to you. I am hoping to spend Xmas here and you can be sure you are thought of each day and always. My love does not alter in the least unless it is to get bigger. We had a mail yesterday but no letter from you, I expect you just missed the boat.

Well goodnight darling, I hope you are keeping well and cheerful. I shall come to you some day and soon. The Turks apparently wanted war no more than we did by what we have found here.

With all my love, Always your own Norman.

Extracts from Norman's Diary

Dec 20 Thursday	*no entry.*
Dec 21 Friday	*Went on fatigué at Wilkins dump morning and afternoon.*
Dec 22 Saturday	*Hear that we are moving. Went with Linzell and 4 men and a Turk round the town of Hebron. Saw Jacob's and Abraham's mosques, the pool of Sarah, Turkish School. The pool where David and Saul fought and where Absolam was hanged. Bought some glass rings made here and an Arab knife. The town is all underground passages and is very dirty.*
Dec 23 Sunday	*Left Hebron. Marched through Wadi el Arab to Bwak (Kilo 11) arriving 8.30. Here are reservoirs made by Solomon in a large gorge. Bivouacked here and it was very cold.*

Sunday 23rd Dec 1917 [postmarked 25th Dec 1917]

My own dearest one,

I am sorry to say I am feeling rather down today. I like to tell you but you mustn't let my folks know because they are older and do not understand that I can be quite well and yet fed up rather. We were really very comfortable in this fine old town – I have just written a letter home telling them all about the sights so you will read that – and we have now orders to move again. Just at Xmas it seems such a pity but I must be brave and cheerful and all will come right in the end. At the base of everything I have your love and you can't tell what a tremendous help that is to me as I have told you before. When I am feeling like I do now I have only to turn to your photo and then I know that there is a great joy in store for me and we must hope that it is nearer than it appears at present. One thing you can be sure of and that is your husband won't grumble at anything he has to put up with as long as you are there to help him through.

I mustn't meet trouble half way I know, but in a day's time we have Xmas day and I must say I rather dread it – I can't see how it will be a merry one or one of peace – but by the time you get this letter many things will have happened and let us pray they may seem a bit sunnier than they look now. I feel a coward writing like this but perhaps I am a bit off colour or something, anyway don't worry and all will be well. I do wish some enterprising gent would finish the war, at times it seems as though it will last for ever and then we get glorious rumours of an early peace. We are starting out for a long march north now and we shall be joining the Herefords, who are about 26 miles from here, tomorrow I expect. I shall be glad for some things to be back with them again and I am hoping there will be some letters from you for me there as it seems a long while since I had one. We are going into the most interesting part of the country now but being under just one canvas sheet at night will be a bit chilly. By the time you read this I hope we shall be in billets again so please dearest don't worry about me at all, I shall be quite alright wherever I am and shall come back to you soon I hope. I <u>do</u> love you but at times I feel I want you so very much, I get out of patience with everything and wonder if there is any good left in the world. I know it is a sign of weakness and I hope you don't get similar feelings but through it all never once have I doubted your love or felt mine waver in the least. Whatever happens my love will never change and I feel confident yours won't although I am not worth such a wife as you will be. I must go now dearest, I am sorry this letter is a cowardly one but I am trying to be brave but I can't forget last Xmas – cheerio there's next Xmas though and what a time we will have then.

You have all my love for ever as you know so I will finish this now hoping I shall cheer you up more in my next letter.
Your very own Norman.

Goodnight dearest I love you more than I can tell, I shall always be true never fear.

With all my love

Always your very own

Norman.

1st Herefordshires

53rd Division

E.E.F.

A typically loving ending to Norman's letters.

[For young men, brought up on the Bible, the Holy Land was something to write home about. This is illustrated by Norman's next diary entries and his letter of 25th, as well as references in his earlier letters to Biblical places, which give a hint as to where he was.]

Extracts from Norman's Diary

Dec 24 Monday Xmas Eve	*Marched through Bethlehem to Jerusalem. Went to service at St. George's Cathedral. A most impressive service.*
Dec 25 Tuesday Xmas Day	*Poured in torrents and was Orderly Officer. Went to St. Stephen's Monastery to sleep owing to wet and had a good Xmas dinner.*
Dec 26 Wednesday	*Visited Jerusalem. Saw the Jaffa Gate, Stations of the Cross, Temple of Omar, Holy Sepulchre, RC Church, Caiaphas House where Christ was betrayed, Pilate's house, Garden of Gethsemane, Mount of Olives. Armenian Church – Dead Sea Jews wailing place. We are just ordered to relieve the Welsh in the trenches tonight. Arrived near Mount of Olives at 7pm and could not sleep owing to extreme cold.*
Dec 27 Thursday	*Had to 'stand to' indefinitely – Some heavy shelling and a fight is going on in the valley.*

[Counter assaults and sporadic fighting continued in the hills around Jerusalem, even though the Turks had surrendered Jerusalem on the 9th December.]

Canaan
Xmas Eve [Monday. But postmarked 31st Dec 1917]

My own beloved,

I have just received your most welcome and cheerful letter. It is absolutely lovely to know for certain that there is such a lovely girl all my very own and waiting until I return. I can't tell you quite where I am but look up hymn 228. [Hymns Ancient and Modern no.228 begins with the word Jerusalem] I joined the battalion today after marching through the most marvellous country, all gorges, precipice roads etc. We camped at the very spot where the wise men of the east slept the night before their entry to see Christ and we followed their footsteps through all this beautiful land. We had a lovely day to continue our march today and are arrived at our destination quite safely. I think tonight – Xmas Eve – I have had the most unique experience anyone can possibly have had. I have attended the first English church service that has been held for 3 years in the cathedral here [St George's Cathedral, Jerusalem] – and for the first time in the history of the world the National Anthem was sung. You really can't realise quite what my feelings were like at such a service. We sang all the Xmas hymns and it was a beautiful church just like St. Michael's at home and I could not believe I was so far from you all.

Later
Xmas Day opened with a perfect deluge of rain, hail and thunder and as we were in very small tents, bivouacs only, you can tell the state I was in. By 8am I had not a dry thing on me and we didn't feel at all as merry as we should have done. This deluge lasted all day and as everyone was in such a state we were put in billets for the night. I was lucky enough to be sent to a Dominican Monastery built on the spot where St. Stephen was stoned. The monks were splendid to us, they all consider us as heroes and they could not do enough for us. The Turks and Germans are absolutely hated by the Christians out here. I had a fine room with a bed and we had a splendid Xmas Dinner at night. Boxing Day was lovely, warm sun and no rain, and I went round all the sights with a Roman Catholic guide – I went into places no visitors are admitted such as the Armenian Convent etc but I am writing a sort of guide book letter which I will send to Father and you will see that.

At present I am in a decent dugout up the line, very comfortable and well fed but very dirty and hard worked. My company clicked by being put in support instead of the front line, so with the exception of snipers and a few shells we are quite peaceful. Luckily the Turk doesn't seem to have many shells to waste so we don't run many risks and you needn't worry at all about me as I am quite safe.

I am very busy and get only about 2 hours sleep a day – none at night usually – but I am very fit and no doubt we shall go back to an easier camp in a few days. This letter is short as my time is very much ditto. I am getting no letters up here and am expecting a huge budget from you all when I return to more peaceful places. Goodnight dearest one, I love you more than ever and I hope you realise it, but I think you do.

With all my love, your very own Norman.
More in my next letter.

SADLY THERE WERE NO MORE LETTERS

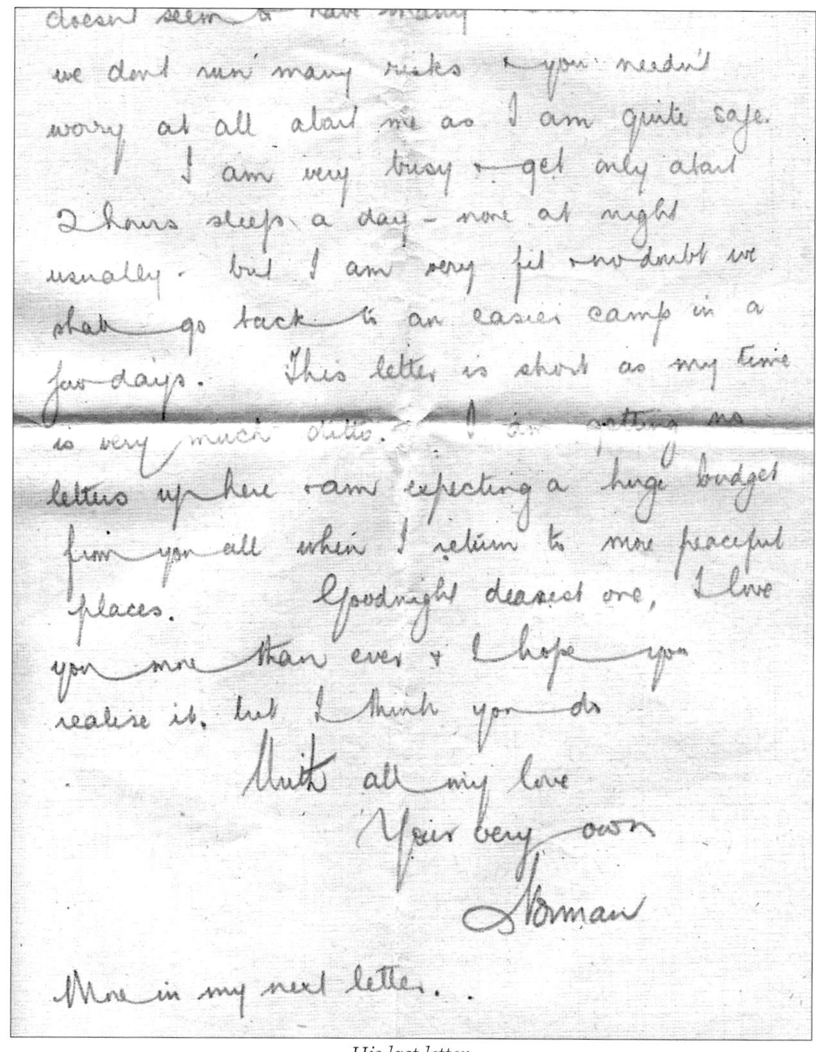

doesn't seem to have many

we don't run many risks & you needn't
worry at all about me as I am quite safe.
I am very busy & get only about
2 hours sleep a day – none at night
usually – but I am very fit & no doubt we
shall go back to an easier camp in a
few days. This letter is short as my time
is very much ditto. I am getting no
letters up here & am expecting a huge budget
from you all when I return to more peaceful
places. Goodnight dearest one, I love
you more than ever & I hope you
realise it, but I think you do

With all my love
Your very own
Norman

More in my next letter..

His last letter.

Norman Albert Wells died of wounds, received on 28th December, on 29th December 1917. He is buried in the Jerusalem War Cemetery, Palestine.

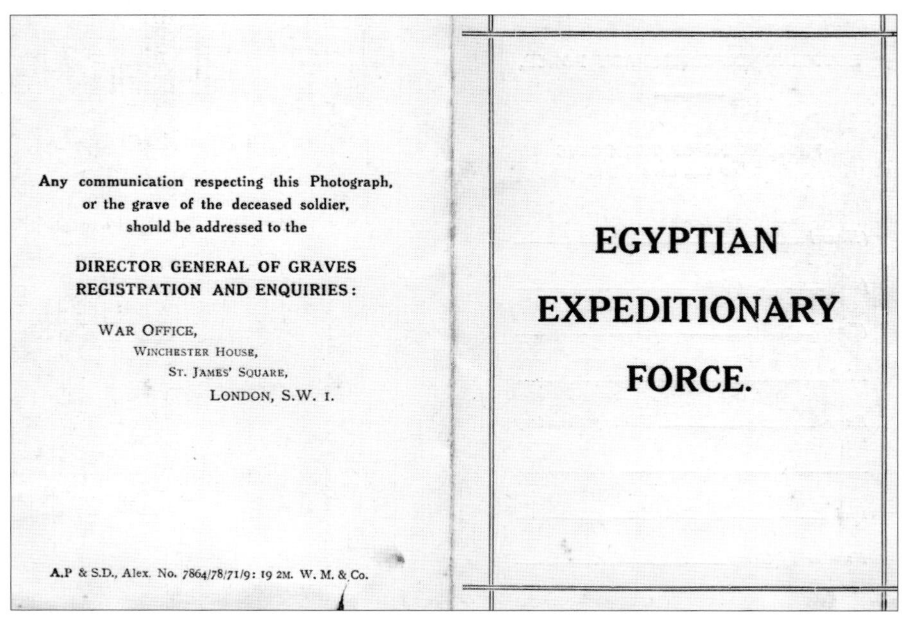

Any communication respecting this Photograph, or the grave of the deceased soldier, should be addressed to the

DIRECTOR GENERAL OF GRAVES REGISTRATION AND ENQUIRIES:

WAR OFFICE,
WINCHESTER HOUSE,
ST. JAMES' SQUARE,
LONDON, S.W. 1.

A.P & S.D., Alex. No. 7864/78/71/9: 19 2M. W. M. & Co.

EGYPTIAN EXPEDITIONARY FORCE.

EGYPTIAN EXPEDITIONARY FORCE.

PHOTOGRAPH OF THE GRAVE OF THE LATE

(Name) Wells N. A.

(No.) (Rank) 2/Lieut

(Unit) 1/1st Bn. Hereford Regt.

Died 29-12-17.

Buried Jerusalem Military Cemetery

Plot S.

Number of Grave 6.

54/51/2037

Official card detailing Norman's grave.

Photo of wooden cross.

Two typed letters were sent, presumably to Norman's father, one explaining how Norman died and the other giving details of his grave.

2nd Welsh Field Ambulance
18th Feb 1918
RAMC (T)

ADMS
53rd Division

2nd Lieut. N A Wells 1/1st Hereford Regiment was admitted to the Italian Hospital, Jerusalem on the 28th December 1917 at which time I was in command of the Hospital. He was brought into Hospital very quickly after being wounded, and was seen at once by Capt. A Pirie Watson, Surgeon Specialist. He had been hit in the abdomen by a shell fragment, and Capt. Pirie Watson asked me to see him in consultation. I found him suffering from considerable shock and collapse, but he was quite conscious and had no pain. He had already had morphia administered to him. I examined his wound and at once corroborated Capt. Watson's opinion that serious internal injury had been caused, and that immediate operation afforded the only chance of saving the patient's life. This was explained to Lieut. Wells and he expressed his willingness to have everything possible done. He took the anaesthetic very well and the operation was only a few minutes' duration. It was found that the liver had been severely injured and that very extensive haemorrhage had already occurred. It was only possible to arrest this temporarily. He regained consciousness completely shortly after the operation, but he slept most of the night and hardly spoke up to the time of his death next day. He died, without any pain, from the effects of haemorrhage. Everything possible was done for him, and he had a nurse in constant attendance from the time of admission until he died. He was buried at the English Cemetery on Mount Zion, and the funeral service was conducted by Canon A Hichens CF who had seen him when he was admitted to hospital. I have no doubt that Canon Hichens would arrange to have a photograph taken of the grave if he were asked. I am now too far from Jerusalem to be able to do anything myself.

W Dunbar, Major, RAMC (TF)

Headquarters,
XX Corps
1st March 1918

Dear Sir,
In reply to your letter Col. Luce is away on leave to England. I have visited the grave with Canon Hichens. We found it at once as it is clearly marked with a cross. Lieut. Wells was buried in the Christian cemetery just outside the walls of Jerusalem on Mount Zion. Standing by the graveside you overlook the beautiful valley of Hinnone south west of the city. Looking westwards you see the low range of hills behind which Bethlehem lies. It is a lovely spot. Sergt. Macdonald RAMC has taken several photographs of it and the surrounding country. The delay in answering your letter is due to the weather. It has been very wet and stormy and we had to wait for a fine day to obtain the photographs. I propose to have this correspondence copied in case it gets lost on the way home.
Yours faithfully,
Frank S Steadman,
Capt. DADMS XX Corps

PS I am keeping the negatives of the photographs here until such time as I hear that the photos have got home safely. Then if Mr Wells likes they will be sent to him.

2nd Lieut. N A Wells, 1/1st Hereford Regt
Admitted Italian Hospital, December 28th 1917

Died of Wounds, December 29th 1917
Date of burial, December 30th 1917
Place of burial, Protestant Cemetery, Mount Zion.
Chaplain, Canon A Hichens.

[In fact, after the British capture of Jerusalem on 9 December 1917 the British army buried its soldiers at Mount Zion Cemetery, before the separate Jerusalem War Cemetery was inaugurated on Mount Scopus in February 1918. A total of 104 British soldiers were buried at Mount Zion, of which 100 were later reburied at the War Cemetery.]

Photo of later headstone.

Photos of Jerusalem War Cemetery.

Rosemary,

The British Military Cemetery, where, outlined against the blue sky, stand, in serried ranks, the crosses of those who died for the peace of Jerusalem.
Fresh flowers had recently been strewn on their graves; flowers from the valley of Koloniah and the hills of Ain Karim; flowers from the fields of Bethlehem & Ramallah and from all the ~~fields~~ places where their feet had trodden.

Envelope that contained rosemary from Jerusalem.

SEC.-LIEUT. AND ADJUTANT NORMAN A. WELLS, Herefords, who died on December 29 from wounds received on the previous day, was the only child of Mr. and Mrs. A. E. Wells, of 12, Trinity Rd., Birchfield, Birmingham. The

lieutenant, who was 27, was well known in local musical circles, having been a member of the Birchfield Amateur Operatic Society for several years, and taking the leading parts in many operas promoted by the society. He was in the service of the National Provincial Bank when the war broke out, and as soon as it was possible to release him he joined, and attained the rank of sergt.-major after twelve months' service. He was then gazetted.

Obituary from local newspaper.

Mr. & Mrs. A. E. Wells desire to express their deep thankfulness for all the Kindly Sympathy extended to them in their great loss.

12, Trinity Road,
Birchfield.

†

NORMAN ALBERT WELLS,

2nd Lieutenant 1st Herefordshire Regt.

Died of Wounds, in Palestine,

December 29th, 1917.

Aged 27.

IN PROUD AND LOVING MEMORY.

"A glorious death is his
Who for his Country falls."

Card from Norman's parents giving thanks for sympathy.

9/Hereford Regiment/460. (Accounts 4.)

This is the Last Will and Testament of me, Norman Albert Wells, of 12 Trinity Road, Birchfields, Birmingham. I bequeath the sum of One hundred pounds, all my pictures, china, and camera to Amiel Robins, of 191 Holly Road, Handsworth, Birmingham if she, at the time of my death is still engaged to me.

All the remainder of my property, money, insurance money, army grants and personal effects to my Mother; and in the event of the above Amiel Robins not being engaged to me at the time of my death all that due to her & mentioned above to go to my Mother.

This Will is made in the Field with the Egyptian Forces on the fifteenth day of November, nineteen hundred and seventeen.

Norman A. Wells

Certified true copy.

A. Bolitho

for the Assistant Financial Secretary

War Office. S.W..

Norman's Will.

NORMAN'S CHRONOLOGY

December 1916 to March 1917	Newmarket, Suffolk. Officer cadet training.
17 April 1917	Appointment in the London Gazette: Territorial Force. Promoted to 2nd Lieutenant on 28 March.
May	Oswestry, Shropshire, Park Hall Camp. 3/1st Hereford Battalion. Amiel and her Mother stayed at Whittington nearby.
June	Altcar near Liverpool. Western Command School of Musketry.
July	Swansea, Singleton Park, Sketty. 3/1st Hereford Battalion merges with the 4th Reserve Battalion of the King's Shropshire Light Infantry.
August	Oswestry on a course, no details but guessing he stayed at 26 Ferrers Road, Oswestry.
October	Joins the 1st Herefordshires, 53rd Division of the Egypt Expeditionary Force. Sails overnight from Southampton to Cherbourg in France on the SS Queen Alexandria (narrowly avoiding submarines). Travels to St. Germain, over the Alps to Firenze (Florence).

Sails from Taranto, Italy, to Alexandria in Egypt.
Is in Kantara, then Karim – detail camp for 53rd Division.

Other places mentioned include:
Beersheba – Hereford reserve camp on rocky hill.
Tel el Sarkarti, Wadi Magir and Auja.
Hebron – where he had a decent billet in a house.
Bethlehem and Jerusalem.

SOLDIERS MENTIONED BY NORMAN

In his letters and diary Norman refers to his army colleagues by surname only, so these identities are suggestions only.

Shaw – training at Newmarket.

Mogridge – probably Captain Edward Cole Mogridge.

Lieutenant Bulmer – possibly Henry Howard Bulmer?

Chubb – Claude Sydney Chubb?

Raymond – Robert Raymond?

Trumper – Francis Algernon Trumper?

Collins – Basil Stratford Collins?

Lewis –

Raylor –

Linzell – Ernest Lincoln Linzell, Royal Welsh Fusiliers?

Wilmot –

Rooks –

Moody –

Lloyd – shares room with Norman in Altcar.

Knapp – Stanley Evelyn Knapp, Gazetted on 27th January 1916. Awarded Military Cross.

Boyce – Eric Arthur

Price – injured right arm, and I think the son of Price working in Amiel's N&P Bank in Birmingham.

Levason – Desmond George Grenville Levason, killed 27th March 1917, buried in the Gaza War Cemetery. Norman visited his widow and parents-in-law while at Altcar.

MRS ROBIN'S RECIPE FOR MARROW JAM

[see letter dated 19th November]

6lbs marrow.
5lbs sugar.
2 lemons.
2 oz bruised ginger (or 1tsp powdered ginger).
1 drachm [a unit of weight formerly used by apothecaries] of chillies tied in muslin bag.

Method. Prepare the day before: peel the marrow and cut into cubes; slice and chop the lemons or grate the rind and squeeze the juice. Put in a bowl all the marrow, lemon and sugar and stand for 24 hours. Next day: place the above ingredients in a preserving pan with the ginger and chillies and cook for 1 hour. Remove the chillie bag and boil slowly until clear and setting (test in a cold saucer) – takes about another half an hour. A jam funnel is essential for pouring into jam jars.

THE GIRLS WHO SANG IN 'THE ALLIES' TROUPE

Music Director – Mr Griffin.
England & Burlington Bertie – Amiel Robins.
Jack Tar (Sailor) – Madge Griffin.
Tommy Atkins (Soldier) – Edie Durban.
Belgium – Beryl Stokes.
France – Ethel Hill.
Italy – Dorothy Durban (pianist).
Russia – Gwen Cattell.
Serbia – Gladys Marson.

AFTERWORD

It is impossible to imagine the grief and loss that Amiel felt on hearing of Norman's death. Her parents and many friends would have suffered with her. If you think how long it took for letters to arrive from such a faraway country, almost a month, Amiel must have been receiving letters from Norman long after he had been killed. What a heartache. My cousin Chris Craig told me that he remembered hearing her saying, many years ago when he was a child, that 'war was a terrible thing' and that she had 'lost a great love in the First World War'. He said that it had stuck in his mind 'as Granny was generally jolly but also somewhat formidable'. He found it a rare display of adult vulnerability. He had also wondered in his childish way how Grandad might have felt about her having had a lost love before he had known her.

In September 1918, Amiel and her parents were holidaying at the Craig-y-don Hotel in Llandudno where they met a Robert Craig from Glasgow. The story goes that he took a great fancy to Amiel but felt that he was far too old for her. A week later he returned and introduced his younger brother Bertie (Herbert). This obviously worked as we're now talking about my Grandfather. Over the following three years Bertie wrote to Amiel regularly. I have another box of letters to read but that will have to be another story. But there was one from Amiel to Bertie, written on New Year's Eve, six months before their wedding. Bertie must have requested that she leave behind her mementoes of Norman once they were married. Amiel wrote:

> 'Darling, you know that I love you above all men and therefore I know jealousy did not prompt the question. The only other motive is a little pride, isn't that so dear? You are afraid your friends might think things. I quite understand Beloved, but does it really matter if they know that I had a friend that neither of us want quite forgotten.'
>
> 'I swear to you that they shall never know more and you need never have the least doubt that I shall not show them how much I love and respect you.'
>
> 'I want to be so at one with you on this point dear because it would really rather hurt, to feel my husband's sympathies were not entirely with me, and

that my old associations had to be so ruthlessly thrust aside, not so much for his sake, (as he trusted me, as you do Love, don't you?) but for his friends.'

This situation will have been repeated many times around the country as a result of the huge loss of life during the First World War. Many husbands may have felt that they were second best. First loves were perhaps more important in those days and maybe we are more careless with our love today.

Amiel and Bertie married at St Michael's Church, Handsworth in June 1921. They started married life in Carnforth, where Bertie was Secretary at Carnforth Haematite Iron Company. In 1925 they moved to Millom, on the coast of Cumbria, where Bertie was commercial manager of the Millom and Askam Iron Co. Ltd. In 1934 Bertie was appointed general manager of the Llanelly [sic] Steel Company (1907) Ltd in South Wales, and so the family moved to Llanelli.

Amiel kept in touch all this time with Norman's parents because in 1938 they came to stay with her and her family in Llanelli. There are photographs of each of them with my mother, aged 10, on a visit to Langland Bay (where, if you remember, Norman suggested it would be lovely for a honeymoon). Amiel and her children enjoyed many holidays at the Brynfield Hotel in Langland during the Second World War because, with petrol rationing and her husband being tied up with work at the Llanelli steelworks, it was not so far to travel to. As a result of which, when my own parents came to move from Llanelli to Swansea, Langland was already a familiar place and they looked to settle there. And, to use Norman's words – it is still a topping place.

Photo of (L-R) Mrs Wells, Amiel's 10 year old daughter Maureen, and mother Mrs Robins, taken at Langland Bay near Swansea in 1938.

SELECTED SOURCES/REFERENCES

Books:
Testament of Youth – Vera Brittain.

Newspapers:
The Guardian 28.09.1979.
Herald of Wales 28.07.1917 (via www.newspapers.library.wales).

Original Sources:
Letters from Norman Wells.
1917 diary kept by Amiel Robins.
Amiel's copy of Norman's Diary for October – December 1917.
Amiel's Autograph Book.
Family photograph collection.

Websites:
Centenary News – centenarynews.com
Commonwealth War Graves Commission – www.cwgc.org
Herefordshire Light Infantry Museum – herefordshirelightinfantrymuseum.com
Imperial War Museum – iwm.org.uk
The Long, Long Trail – www.longlongtrail.co.uk
thewittercollection.co.uk